I'LL GO

Reflections From My 61 Years of
Ministry On How to Question, Follow
and Lead

DOUGLAS NORRIS

ISBN-13:978-1494757656
ISBN-10:1494757656

All profits from the sale of this book will be contributed to the Douglas and Eleanor Norris Scholarship Fund at Garrett-Evangelical Theological Seminary, 2121 Sheridan Road, Evanston, Illinois 60201.

DEDICATED TO

Alison

Adrienne

Erin

Julia

Melanie

Sara

Amanda

Tyler

Our gifted, loving, energetic grandchildren who, in their own ways, are hearing and answering the Call to go . . . *love God and serve.*

ACKNOWLEDGEMENTS

Who, me? Write a book?

My dear wife Ellie nudged, "Go for it," so I decided, "I'll go . . . write a book." We have had and are having adventure upon adventure with unusual experiences unique to my ministry so why not share and, hopefully, inspire.

Why God called me into the pastoral ministry I do not know, but I am eternally grateful. And I'm humbly appreciative of the congregations who labored with me—sometimes reluctantly, but most of the time joyfully and expectantly. Thank you.

I am also deeply indebted to:

- my wife Eleanor (Ellie) who in faith and love has been at my side since 1958 and who has proved to be an excellent editor;

- Jack and Craig for editing with very helpful comments;

- granddaughter Sara for her drawing at age 9 which is now the cover design;

- granddaughter Alison for graphics and formatting the cover;

- granddaughter Adrienne for expanding the vision of the book;

- Tim, Jennifer and Laura for their comments, suggestions and encouragement; and

- Robert Bartron for his expertise, advice and encouragement. An excellent author, you can read about him and his books on mcavepublishing.com.

FOREWORD

Unforgettable, unbelievable, laughable, inspiring, unusual, tragic events in my 61 years of ministry—all the while singing the gospel song, "*I'll go where you want me to go, dear Lord*"—I have had an incredible journey broadening my perspective, outlook, world-view and theology.

I believe the Lord calls all of us to "go." Go is a signature theme of the Bible. The Lord said to Abraham, the father of our faith, Genesis 12.1, "*Go from your country to the land that I will show you.*" The Lord said to Moses in Exodus 3:7,10, "*I have heard my people cry in their slavery. Go to Egypt, confront the Pharaoh, and lead my people to freedom.*" The Lord said to Amos in Amos 7.14, "*Leave your herds, leave your sycamore trees, and go preach to my people Israel.*" Jesus said to his disciples in Matthew 28.19, "*Go and make disciples of all nations.*"

The events and commentary in this book cover a ministry of over 61 years.

Table of Contents

INTRODUCTION

"I'll Go" is a recurring theme in my life, and I've been blessed living in great communities and working with very special churches. This book shares some of what I've learned and some of the stories that have touched my life.

Early years

I grew up on a small dairy farm 25 miles north of Minneapolis. We had 12 cows, and each had a name. My childhood was very happy, lonely at times as the only neighbor near my age was a girl three years older than I with whom I occasionally played. The nearest town was St. Francis, 3½ miles to the north. On the Rum River, it had two churches (Methodist and Baptist), two grocery stores, two beer joints, a blacksmith shop and a school. I attended grades 1-12, except for the third, which I skipped, in one building. There was no kindergarten class. The high school was on the third floor; hence, the name "high school."

There were only 30 in my graduating class, but the small size of the school afforded me many opportunities. I played trombone in the band, sang in the chorus, was editor of the mimeographed school paper, president of the student council, debated on the debate team, and had the lead role in two three-act plays. Notice, no athletics, but I was scorekeeper for the basketball team, which did not win a game in my six years of junior and senior high school! We learned patience, perseverance and fortitude, and we never gave up!

My Dad had rebelled against his strict Baptist upbringing, and my Mother's family was unchurched, so we didn't go to church. However, my Grandpa Norris took me to the Baptist Church in my preschool years until he was unable to drive. One Sunday, Grandma, knowing how Grandpa missed going to church, asked him to join her and listen to a radio religious program. He ambled into the bedroom, rummaged around in a drawer, found his "hated" hearing aids, put them in his ears, returned to the living room, sat down and asked what they were listening to. She replied, "Rev. George Mecklenberg from Wesley Methodist Church." "Methodist!" he fumed, got up, went back into the bedroom, and threw his hearing aids into the drawer!

However, when I was in sixth grade, a neighbor invited me to go to the Methodist Church with her and her children. There, in a one room building with a basement and a loving congregation where the old folks called me "Dougie," I found Jesus, who had already found me, and I was baptized.

In high school, I was very active in the youth group and taught a Sunday School class in the basement kitchen. Our youth group often conducted services in the nursing home and neighboring churches. I was the preacher. While a freshman at the University of Minnesota, I came home every weekend and was Superintendent of the Sunday School.

During this time, I felt God calling me into the ministry. Singing *"I'll go where you want me to go, dear Lord,"* I transferred to Hamline University in St. Paul for my sophomore year.

What follows are reflections from my 61 years of ministry and what I've learned on how to question, follow and lead.

CHAPTER 1

Tell Them About Yeesus

Who, me?

I was only 18 years old when the District Superintendent asked me to pastor two churches. It was a hot, humid afternoon in St. Paul, and I was attending the closing session of the Minnesota Annual Conference of The Methodist Church. (In 1968, when the Methodist Church merged with the Evangelical United Brethren Church, the name was changed to United Methodist). The Bishop and Superintendents had not completed the appointments of ministers to churches, so we sat in the sanctuary of Hamline Methodist Church (on the campus of Hamline University) singing hymns and waiting for the appointments to be announced.

Methodists practice the itinerant system, where pastors rotate. A bishop, in collaboration with district superintendents, appoints ministers to churches for one year. At the end of the year, the minister may be reappointed or moved to another church.

It was fascinating to watch a superintendent come into the sanctuary and walk down the aisle, looking for a particular pastor. When he found the one he wanted, he beckoned to him (the superintendents and pastors were all men in 1952). The beckoned pastor followed him into the "back room" while the rest murmured, wondering where they were going to send that pastor.

Finally, the hymn singing ended. The Bishop and superintendents entered and the appointments were read. This was in mid-June. By July 1, ministers and families had moved out of their parsonages and moved into the home of their new appointment. The congregations had little time to say goodbye. On the last Sunday of June, they bade farewell and on the first Sunday of July greeted their new pastor!

(This unbelievable system has now been changed. Bishops and superintendents now take months to make appointments: talking to churches and pastors, arranging for interviews and announcing where each is going before the Annual Conference meets in session.)

After the session was over, Ed Foote, the Central District Superintendent, approached me and asked if I would consider being appointed to Cedar and West Bethel Churches. There were not enough ordained pastors to serve all the churches so special appointments were made. Persons such as I were given special authorization to pastor on a part-time basis. I was allowed to preach, baptize and serve Communion, while still going to school. I was then a sophomore at Hamline University.

With fear, trepidation, anxiety, but full of faith and the courage to go "where angels fear to tread," I responded, "I'll go!"

The two Minnesota rural churches—Cedar in a small village and West Bethel in open country, were about 12 miles from my parents' home. I sang, *"I'll go where you want me to go, dear Lord,"* but it wasn't long before I realized what I had gotten myself into. My predecessor had a difficult time, especially in one of the churches. In fact, only three people came to church on his farewell Sunday!

One Saturday afternoon I visited a neighboring pastor of another denomination, an old man full of years and wisdom. I told him the situation and asked, "What do I, 18-years-old, wet behind the ears, with more courage than sense, preach to my elders? Why will they listen to me?" I can still see him, leaning back in his chair, folding his hands over his ample stomach, looking me squarely in the eyes, and saying in his heavy Dutch accent, "Tell them about Yeesus! They won't dare pick a fight with Jesus! Tell them the old, old story of Jesus and his love."

I followed his advice. What an unforgettable three years I had in those churches! Sunday worship attendance soon grew to 50 in each church, with 25 in each youth group. I've often felt that all youth leaders should be 18-21 years old! We went on retreats, haunted abandoned houses, conducted Vacation Bible School for children and went on excursions. Many Sunday evenings, we went to neighboring church services or to Minneapolis. We went to Billy Graham rallies and Sister Fern extravaganzas. I recall one revival when the pastor introduced the offering by saying, "It costs us 15 cents to rent each chair." Jim said, "I only have a nickel, so I'll only sit on 1/3 of the chair." I was afraid we'd get kicked out trying to smother our laughter.

And then there were none!

On one Father's Day, I prepared a humdinger of a sermon for fathers—easy since I wasn't one yet! But, in West Bethel Church, there were no fathers there. It was the opening day of the fishing season! I learned quickly how to adapt, improvise and wipe my brow!

My sermons were well received. "Don't let seminary take away your fire!" was the frequent admonition.

I met Ellie

I made lifetime friends at Hamline including beautiful, vivacious Eleanor Smith who in 1952 was crowned Stillwater Snow Queen and with 31 other city snow queens represented Stillwater for a week as a guest of the St. Paul Winter Carnival. We had fun together at Hamline, lunched at noon in the Student Union, laughed a lot and almost got kicked out of the library for giggling!

Most of our dates were trips to one of my churches for special events, a round trip of 100 miles. On one trip I drove through a snow storm and hit a patch of ice. The car rotated 360 degrees, ending up in a ditch in a farm yard. The farmer graciously pulled us out. Our marriage has continued to be filled with adventure!

CHAPTER TWO

Go Where? Jesus said, "Go Into All the World" (Mark 16:15)

Growing up in white rural Minnesota, I lived in isolation. The first and only black family moved into our neighborhood while I was in high school. The "other religion" was Roman Catholic! There were no Jews, no Muslims and only one Mormon family. But, the Lord took me on journeys to other lands, other races, other religions and other cultures—incredible growing experiences.

I often preached about missions, challenging the congregations to reach out beyond their walls, recalling John Wesley (the founder of Methodism) who preached, "The world is my parish."

And I listened to my own sermons. One day a representative from the Board of Missions visited Hamline's campus and spoke about the denomination's 3-year short-term missionary program. I told Ellie about it. She said, "You're going, aren't you?" I sang, *"I'll go where you want me to go, dear Lord,"* and, following graduation, off I went to Nashville, Tennessee for six-weeks of missionary training before being sent to Nagoya, Japan as a three-year short-term missionary. Being single was a requirement.

Returning from Nashville, I was invited to preach the next Sunday in Wisconsin. I phoned and invited Ellie to go with me, but she was driving three college friends to Canada for the weekend. Expecting to be home for a few more weeks, I promised to call when she returned on Tuesday.

But, not wanting to miss my call, she drove home a day early. She waited for my phone call on Tuesday; she waited on Wednesday. By the end of the week, she received a letter I mailed from Amarillo, Texas! The Board of Missions suddenly found a freighter to take me to Japan from San Francisco, and had me board a train immediately. Without answering machines or voice mail in those days, it was impossible to let Ellie know I had gone.

The next time we saw each other was when I returned from Japan three years later—a month before our well-planned wedding.

I'll go . . . to Nagoya

After a few days in San Francisco, I sailed to Japan aboard a freighter. There were 12 passengers, and when I wasn't seasick (about half the time) we had a good time playing cards and making fudge!

After the two week trip, I arrived in Yokohama, was met and taken to the train to go to Nagoya, the third largest city in Japan. Nagoya, still rebuilding after the war (this was 1955), was hustling and bustling with tall buildings, department stores and an enviable transportation system. And, people! When boarding a light rail, an attendant's sole job was to push the passengers into the train so the door could shut. I was grateful for my height! My head was above the mob. But, everyone was quiet, polite and friendly.

Nagoya Gakuin

I was a teacher of English Conversation at Nagoya Gakuin, a Methodist junior and senior high boys' school. I shared the missionary house, located on a corner of the campus, with Roger Floyd who was from Connecticut. We had a live-in housekeeper who prepared our meals, did our laundry and took care of us royally.

There were 1800 students in the school, 60 in a classroom. Roger and I shared the English Conversation teaching, each teaching 15 hours a week. The first year I had five 8th grade classes, five 9th grade classes and five 11th grade classes. In total, I taught 900 students; each class one hour a week. As there was no prepared curriculum, Roger helped me develop my lesson plans. Japanese teachers taught English grammar, reading and writing. Roger and I taught pronunciation and conversation.

Unlike American schools, the students stayed in their rooms, and the teachers rotated. There was a large teachers' room where we each had our own desks. As grading was done using numbers, I learned how to use an abacus, and became quite adept at it! Looking back, I don't know how I did it—900 students!

After school, I held Bible classes, teaching in English. Many students were very motivated to learn English.

Chuo Kyokai

On Sundays, I went to Central Church (Chuo Kyokai) in downtown Nagoya, worshiped in the morning, and taught an English Bible class in the evening before the evening service. I often was the organist, pumping the foot pedals.

Usually five or six boys accompanied me to morning worship. I learned how to read the words used in the hymnal, so I sang with gusto, and learned how to be attentive to the sermon without understanding it. I learned enough Japanese to have short conversations, order food, ask for directions and remain out of trouble. My conversations with adults brought smiles as I learned from students and, as in the States, teen agers have their own language.

Hit the road

Japanese love to travel, and so do I! Excursions were an important part of the school's program. Each grade took trips lasting several days. 300 boys lined up at train stations, and off we went. As one of the resident foreigners, I was often invited. I went on my first trip a few weeks after I arrived and slept on the floor in hotels on futons. I found the food quite different from Minnesota meat and potatoes! Rice and fish didn't fill me up, especially having difficulty getting the food into my mouth with chopsticks, and I came back to Nagoya quite hungry! But, I soon learned how to master chopsticks and relish the food!

On one trip to Tokyo, we passed Mt. Fuji. As I had yet to see the famous mountain, I anxiously awaited the view; but, again, it was foggy and rainy. In my usual style, I complained loudly about the weather, until one student quietly said, "Sensei, the rain comes down from sky, not from the ground up, and there is nothing we can do about it!" That shut me up!

I took several boys on a bike trip, making camp wherever we could find space, cooking our own food and having a wonderful time.

Ouch!

A tooth was causing great pain, so I took it to a dentist. With the language barrier, I didn't understand what he was doing. I learned later that he had performed my first root canal without anesthesia! I kept sliding down in the chair until I was almost on the floor. He said, "You Mericans no like pain!" I guess not!

New arrangements

Roger's three-year term was up a year after I arrived. He was replaced by Ben and Lily Sawada and their daughter, Kathy. They moved into the missionary house, and I moved into the teachers' apartment building. There were four families and four single bachelors. We shared the kitchen, toilet and ofuro (bath).

The ofuro is like our hot tubs, but made of wood. Using a small tin bowl, I soaped and rinsed before getting into the scalding, hot water—relaxing, renewing. In winter, I went to bed warm! In hotels, the ofuro was shared, but I bathed alone in the apartment building, waiting for my turn. In one hotel, I shared the ofuro (large like a small swimming pool) with several elderly women. We politely pretended we didn't see each other.

I ate breakfasts with the custodian couple in their apartment on the school grounds. Wonderful folks who didn't understand English so we communicated with my poor, student language. Breakfast usually included fish, rice and misoshiru soup with a raw egg dropped into it. Delicious!

For lunch, I ordered from a restaurant and ate in the teachers' room with the other teachers. The food came in bento boxes made of bamboo, stacked high on the back of a bicycle. Hot, delicious green tea was available all day long.

For dinner, I ate in the missionary house with the Sawada family. During my third year, a second baby girl, Mariellen, was born. Fifty years later, our paths crossed again after I responded "I'll go…."

Chapter Three

What About Other Religions?

If one worships God under any name, one worships the one God, for there is but one God. There are many ways of perceiving God, of experiencing God, of naming God, of worshiping God, but they all point to the one God. For example, the Golden Rule appears in all the major religions. Most of the religions teach, "Don't do to others what you don't want done to you," but Jesus made it proactive, "Do to others as you would have them do to you." There are many deeply spiritual non-Christians. Mahatma Gandhi was a spiritual giant, and Gandhi was a Hindu.

In Romans 1:19-20, Paul wrote that ever since the creation of the world, God's eternal power and divine nature have been understood and experienced through what God has made. People throughout history have similar consciences and instinctively know right from wrong.

There are also differences among the religions, and we need to recognize that development and growth occur in understanding God. Some of the earlier religions practiced sacrifice—animals, and in some places, humans. Early in the Bible, human sacrifice was repudiated. Some wonder why God would ask Abraham to sacrifice his son, Isaac.

But, the point of the incident is that God stopped Abraham from sacrificing Isaac, and human sacrifice was never part of the Jewish or Christian religions.

How should Christians relate to other religions?

The traditional stance of Christians towards other religions has been **adversarial**.

Pope Alexander VI told the Spanish and Portuguese to convert natives or if they refused to be converted, conquer, enslave or exterminate them. Pioneers treated the American Indians in the same way.

Protestant missionaries treated people of other religions as objects to be converted, believing that Christians are superior and that heaven only has room for Christians. A young man I've known since he was a child wrote me. His mother had recently remarried and was now a Buddhist. The minister of a large student group at Cal Poly, San Luis Obispo, told the young man that his mother was now going to hell. I wrote back and told him, "Tell that minister to go to hell, and you go find a church that preaches the love of Jesus!" What arrogance to think Christians have an exclusive claim on God, sending 2/3 of the world to hell!

An opposite stance is what I call **Inoffensive Mush**. You've probably heard it. "There are many roads that lead to God. Christianity is one of the roads. As long as you are sincere and live a good life, one religion is as good as another." This stance melts all religions down into inoffensive mush with sincerity as the criterion of a true worshiper. But, what about those who are sincerely wrong? I suspect Hitler was quite sincere!

Let me suggest an alternative stance to **Adversarial** and **Inoffensive Mush**. I call it the **Partner** stance. The global problems that face humankind—climate change, moral decay, injustice, AIDS, hunger, war, fighting between religions and fighting within religions —take more than just Christians to solve. We need each other. Let's enter into partnership, beginning by appreciating what the other religions can bring to the table, what they can teach us, and then work together to solve some problems.

A Wesley Church member was two hours from death when he entered the hospital. He credits his miraculous progress in part to spiritual experiences, beginning with a visit from Rev. Motoe. She listened, prayed and then sang "Amazing Grace." He said he could feel angels in the room. He had nurses who prayed with him and one of his doctors sat by his bed, held his hand and prayed out loud. The doctor! The doctor told Dale that he had a team of spiritual doctors who were concerned and who prayed for their patients, three in particular—a Hindu, a Muslim and a Christian! Why can't we get along with other religions? Why can't we appreciate one another? Why can't we partner and save human lives? Is it fear? Is it prejudice? Of course there are extremists—violent, fundamentalist radicals, even in Christianity; but let's learn how to relax, appreciate and cooperate with other religions.

Partner—appreciate, cooperate and share. As Christians, we share our faith, not in judgment, not from a superior to inferior position, but humbly and respectfully. We go in the name of Christ to build buildings, heal the sick, feed the hungry, teach the children. As we minister in Jesus' name, we tell our story. We tell them about Jesus. We tell them how we know God through Jesus, how we have experienced the love of God through Jesus. As partners, we don't hide our faith. We gladly share, and we gladly listen to their stories.

The Partner stance is the best stance for missionaries to take towards other religions, beginning with respect.

When a Buddhist dies

One Sunday morning in Japan, the Principal called and said one of the teachers had died so he and other dignitaries must go immediately to pay their respects to the family, and would I drive the car? We were met at the door by the widow and son. Black cloths were hanging everywhere and there were many flowers. In the living room, there was a beautiful large Buddhist altar. Buddhist funerals are held in the homes. (Most Japanese go to the Shinto shrines to be married and have Buddhist funerals when they die).

I watched carefully so as to be able to imitate. We bowed and bowed while the widow told of the circumstances regarding his death. Then we went into the altar room. One at a time, we went up to the altar, knelt on a pillow facing the altar, clasped our hands and bowed two times to it. On the return we bowed to the family.

The funeral was the next day. Again, I watched what the others did. There was a table in the entry with the family kneeling by it. One at a time we went up to the table, took two pinches of incense, dropped them in the burner, bowed towards the altar room, bowed to the family and went outside. I wanted to go inside to see the service as priests in beautiful orange robes were chanting, but because there was such a crowd, we school people did not enter. After the service, there was a procession to the crematorium which did not include us.

*   *   *

Our Wesley Church in San Jose has a respectful, amicable relationship with the Buddhist Church down the street. They borrow items from each other; they attend each other's fundraisers, and the Wesley Jazz Band often plays at their dances. Both of the churches are active in Japantown activities. They respect each other and look for ways to cooperate and share.

CHAPTER FOUR

I'll Go . . . to Garrett

When my three-year term in Nagoya was completed, the Board of Missions no longer used freighters, so I flew from Tokyo to Seattle. My folks, along with Ellie and my sister Mary, pulled their 13-foot trailer and had a leisurely sight-seeing trip on the way. I don't remember how five of us slept in that trailer! Besides us, Bill and Dorothy, good friends from West Bethel Church, which I pastored in college, joined us for a few days. They also slept in the trailer! It was Ellie's adventure to become fully acquainted with her in-laws for two weeks just a few weeks before our wedding.

A month after I returned from Japan, Eleanor June Smith and I were married in Trinity Lutheran Church in Stillwater, Minnesota.

After a four-day honeymoon in northern Minnesota where one side trip landed us in a municipal dump on the Gunflint Trail, we immediately moved to Evanston, Illinois where three years later I earned a Master of Divinity degree from Garrett Theological Seminary (the name changed to Garrett-Evangelical when it merged with the Evangelical Theological Seminary in 1974). Ellie taught business courses at Evanston Township High School.

During the previous Easter week, Ellie's Dad drove her to Evanston for three interviews in Chicago area schools. Her last interview was at Evanston Township High at 11:00 a.m. They were scheduled to leave for Minnesota at 1:00 p.m., and by then she had been hired and signed the contract to teach business courses beginning August 25.

She also had arranged for a tour of Garrett's newly purchased apartment building being readied for the incoming fall class. The delightful, retired pastor manager then allowed her to choose our one-room apartment. Every night, the furniture was pushed aside to accommodate the roll-away bed which was stored upright in the closet. The El (elevated train) rattled by but we soon got used to the racket.

Our second year we moved to a one-bedroom apartment. As student housing was limited to two years, for our third year we were fortunate to rent a house (the landlady lived in the basement) just one block from the high school. The first two years I walked to school and Ellie drove; the third year Ellie walked and I drove.

*   *   *

Garrett is on the campus of Northwestern University, both started by Methodists. When I was there, Garrett was located on the shore of Lake Michigan. I enjoyed studying on the lawn overlooking the lake. Now the water is not visible from the Garrett campus. Northwestern filled in a large portion of the lake and built several buildings on the fill between Garrett and the lake. I enjoyed Garrett, made life-long friends, received a good education and was awarded Distinction in Preaching.

CHAPTER FIVE

Strength In Numbers— The Team Approach

When I graduated from seminary, the District Superintendent said, "We're experimenting with rural church ministry and are creating the first cooperative parish in the Minnesota Conference. We are appointing you to four churches in the Central Minnesota Methodist Parish." There were ten churches in the parish with four pastors— Delton Krueger, Mary MacNicholl, Bill Mealio (who was a member of the West Bethel Church when I was pastor) and I. A few months later, a Church and Community Worker, Phyllis Neal, was hired. She was paid by a grant from the denomination's Women's Society.

Delton and Phyllis have each written excellent books: *Portable Guide to World Religions,* by Delton Krueger, and *Questions God Asks in the Hebrew Scriptures*, by Phyllis A. Cooper (formerly Neal). Both books are available on Amazon.com.

Each church elected one woman and one man to represent their church on the Parish Council, where we planned cooperative events and discussed how we might help each other. We pastors often rotated and preached in each other's churches. There was a central office in the

Princeton Church where the weekly bulletins, newsletters, annual reports, etc. were produced. We even designed a parish cover for bulletins. Each pastor, however, planned his or her own order of worship.

The parish idea was to put teamwork into action. Pastoring rural churches as a solo pastor can be a lonely and isolated experience. There is strength in numbers.

Several of us were invited to go to Iowa and share our experience to encourage the Iowa Conference to organize cooperative parishes. When it was my turn to speak, I likened a young pastor coming out of seminary to a boxer. The pastor, after three years of intense study and field work experiences, comes out swinging, dancing with excitement, ready to take on the world, ready to enlist his or her rural church in the fight to "spread scriptural holiness throughout the land," which was the mantra of pioneer Methodists as the Methodist movement spread throughout the country. The pastor comes out swinging but the congregation is sprawling in the corner laid back, wearing no gloves, yawning and muttering, "What's with this guy?"

Such a pastor needs more than a support network; he/she will be more effective on a team where there is more than support, where they work together, not isolated or alone.

Milaca, Estes Brook, Glendorado, Santiago

I was pastor of four of the churches—one in open country, two in very small villages, and the fourth in the county seat town of Milaca, a population of 1,800 where we lived in the parsonage. There were about 25 in worship each week in the three country churches and 100 in Milaca. I held three services on Sunday morning and one in the evening. After preaching the same sermon four times in one day, even I was tired of it! Ellie accompanied me until Jack was born. One snowy Sunday morning, driving our VW Beetle, I hit a snow plow! I can still see the driver shaking his head. I thought the snow flurry was a blizzard!

The parish celebrates

All ten churches combined for special events. In 1962, 250 toured all ten churches in a caravan of bright orange school buses. One parishioner noticed Ellie leaving the little outhouse at several churches and then jumping on the last bus. She was concerned for Ellie's health. "Oh, no" said Ellie, "my job today is to check every rest room before the last bus leaves so no one is left behind!"

In 1964, the gathering featured a giant barbecue. A hole the size of a grave was dug in the grounds of the Glendorado Church (one of my churches). The hole was filled with wood and lit. When all the wood had burned with white coals and a blue gray flare remaining, 1-2 inches of sand were laid. The sand was covered with paper and 500 lbs. of beef in 8-10 lb. packages were laid on top. Sheet metal was placed over the trench and quickly covered with a foot of dirt. The meat cooked overnight on Saturday with men camping out and watching it. What an unforgettable feast and what fun!

On Sunday, 750 parishioners were divided into three groups and led by men carrying flags on a "pilgrimage with Christ." They moved around the grounds to view living tableaux depicting the teaching, preaching and healing ministries of Jesus. Simultaneously at each of the three locations, scenes were reenacted. Actors, readers, singers and instrumentalists in the scenes represented all ten churches.

Following the fabulous barbecue dinner, an outdoor Communion service with 14 loaves of home-made bread, was led by Bishop T. Otto Nall. Following the Communion service, the entire congregation formed a huge heart with confirmation classes forming a cross in the middle. Photos were taken. A Commissioning service ended the day. The Nalls ended the celebration with dinner at our parsonage.

The event was featured with photos and articles in *Together* magazine. A photo of the Communion service appeared on the cover. When our issue arrived, young Jack pointed and exclaimed, "There's Daddy!"

Home Bible Study

Finding no published materials available for home Bible study, we pastors prepared our own correspondence courses. More than 100 persons participated by mail.

"Will the Sunday School teachers please come forward."

It was Christian Education Sunday to kick off the fall program. As I had recently arrived as pastor, I didn't have time to personally speak with each Sunday School

Superintendent so I sent letters informing them that I would be dedicating the teachers. In Estes Brook Church, Bertha, the Superintendent and pianist, sitting in the front row, squirmed, and looked at a woman who shook her head. Then Bertha turned around, pointed to the back and said, "Dena, sometimes you teach; you go up there." Dena replied, "I'm not going up there." I quickly said, "Forget it. Let's dedicate the whole church!" I found out later that the first to come were handed the lesson books, and told to teach.

Erroneous assumption

An elderly couple lived behind the parsonage. We were friendly and when the man was dying, we were neighborly, but I did not offer to pray with them because, you see, they were Lutherans. In Minnesota, if you are not Catholic, you surely are a Lutheran! I had them neatly confined within their little box and didn't want to infringe on their privacy. Little did I know how needy they were until a minister of another church began calling on them. He helped the man overcome his fear of dying, led him to Christ, and comforted the couple with the promise of eternal life. How grateful was the wife! Don't assume anything about anyone. Don't put people in boxes. Don't judge people on the basis of what is fair, but look on people as God loves them.

Marketing

I learned the importance and effectiveness of marketing. Milaca Church held a monthly potluck after the worship service. In Minnesota at that time, there were few fresh fruits or vegetables in the winter so most of the items were jello and spaghetti/tomato hot dishes (called casseroles or covered dishes in other parts of the country). I grew tired of the same menu, so I started calling it a Family Smorgasbord in the monthly newsletter and the Sunday bulletin. And the menu changed! People started bringing ham, meatballs and creative dishes. All because of a word change.

What about church mergers?

Cooperation can't be forced! I was instructed by two District Superintendents to merge the three country churches. After long discussion, two of the three, Glendorado and Estes Brook, agreed to merge; however the woman who ran the Estes Brook Church was so angry she refused to vote. The church merged without her, and she did not participate. The third church, Santiago, led by the woman who ran the church, refused to merge. Mary MacNicholl became pastor of Santiago, along with the three she already had; and I became pastor of Milaca, the newly merged church called Fellowship, and Zimmerman, a small town 25 miles south of Milaca. Bill Mealio, Zimmerman's pastor, left to go to seminary.

After I left, Santiago and Fellowship (the merged churches) closed. So much for church mergers! I learned that small churches are closely knit groups gathered around one leader. The effort to merge is as successful as trying to merge circles in the United Methodist Women! Highly unlikely. When I was in Modesto, I was told that years before a decree came from "on high" that the circles should rotate membership. The younger women were so incensed they quit, and when I arrived there was a circle of older women, a circle of younger women but a huge gap where there should have been a circle of middle-aged women, for they had pulled out years before.

Zimmerman and Milaca

I held worship services in Zimmerman and Milaca on Sunday mornings and in Fellowship Church Sunday evening. The drive returning to Milaca Church, 25 miles from Zimmerman, in time for the 11am service, was a challenge. The District Superintendent accompanied me one Sunday. When we returned to Milaca, he greeted the congregation with a "Whew! Unbelievable! We made it in time." and shortness of breath!

During the five years, my churches changed, but Milaca remained constant and, because we lived in the parsonage, we called Milaca "home."

When it's fun

When a team, a staff, or a committee is working on a proposal or a problem and the result is something no one brought to the meeting, what fun it is!

You must admit that many meetings are boring. What fun it was when the Parish Council brainstormed about how we might cooperate and ideas flowed. No one came to the meeting with the idea of digging a giant hole in the ground and barbecuing beef overnight with all ten churches gathering for dramas and feasting, but that was the happy result.

Creatively working together—setting aside biases, preconceived notions, egos and personal needs—is a rare phenomenon and when it happens, the Holy Spirit is allowed to work. The result is pure joy and satisfaction. Such productivity from creativity requires leaders and participants who are flexible, tolerant, open; who do not insist that their way is the best.

CHAPTER SIX

Dealing With Thorns

In 2 Corinthians 12:7, Paul wrote, *"I was given a thorn in my flesh."* We don't know what the "thorn" was, nor how it affected or hurt Paul, but it didn't stop him from his ministry. In verse 9, he affirmed God's grace—"My grace is sufficient for you."

Helen

Helen joined Merced Church while I was pastor. She had a keen sense of mission—a call to do children's ministry. She taught Sunday School and directed a children's choir while accompanying the choir on the piano.

You might be thinking: what's so special about Helen? Helen was totally blind and also suffered a severe hearing loss. Helen had been a schoolteacher. When she began losing her sight, she studied Braille, and, when I met her, she had a guide dog named Foxie. And, I repeat, Helen taught Sunday School and directed a children's choir.

Every week, Mary Fran, the Sunday School Superintendent, read Helen the next Sunday's lesson so she could prepare the lesson plan. Helen taught the first and second grade class.

She played the piano for the choir and for her Sunday School class with Foxie, her guide dog, lying on the floor. She learned new songs by listening to them on her tape recorder and then played them by ear on the piano. When the children sang in the worship service, sighted persons led the children to the chancel steps while Helen, following Foxie, made her way to the piano. Helen sat at the piano and struck various keys until she found the correct key of the song. The children waited politely, started singing at the proper time and gave a rousing, loud song of praise to the Lord. They were taught to sing loudly so that Helen could hear them! When we were in Merced a few years later, we heard 40 children sing. There was hardly a dry eye in the church.

Helen began both Sunday School and the Tuesday afternoon children's music session by calling the roll. She called out names from memory and learned by their response where each child was sitting. The sighted person who helped her in Sunday School was a male college professor. One Sunday during Sunday School, Helen stopped what she was doing and asked, "Where is William?" Max, the sighted teacher, hadn't even missed William, but Helen knew he was not where he was supposed to be. Max found William hiding behind the piano! Helen may have been blind, but she had eyes in the back of her head.

Helen lived about six blocks from the church and walked to the church. One day Foxie was attacked by an unleashed dog. Both Helen and Foxie were frightened. Our senior high youth group swung into action. They wrote letters to the Chief of Police and the newspaper requesting that the leash laws be enforced. The next Sunday afternoon the youth gathered in Helen's house and then walked her back to the church while praying all along the way that the route would be safe for Foxie and Helen. When they arrived at the church for the youth meeting, Helen stayed and spontaneously gave a moving and inspiring testimony to the power of prayer.

One day Helen and Foxie got on the train by themselves, rode to Oakland, boarded a bus, crossed over the Bay Bridge to San Francisco and were met by a friend. They had lunch. Helen said her husband thinks she is crazy, but he learned years ago not to try to hold her back!

During a Sunday worship service, I blessed Foxie, and, when Foxie became sick, we prayed for her; but the time came for her to be "put down." The guide dog people came from Santa Rosa and took Foxie back with them. I asked Helen if she would like me to be with her, and three of us gathered in Helen's kitchen at the time Foxie was "put down" in Santa Rosa. We prayed and talked about Foxie.

The next Tuesday, I held a Memorial Service for Foxie, the first and only funeral I've had for a dog! We held it after the children's music time. Five guide dogs in training were there! Their trainers, most of whom were teenagers, brought their dogs to the chancel and introduced them. During the Sharing Time, children took turns coming up to the microphone to tell how they loved Foxie. Another day with no dry eyes in the house! Helen was then given a new dog, which required her to go to Santa Rosa for a period of training so that she and the new dog, Caper, could communicate.

Helen recognized voices, and whenever she heard mine she would say, "Give me a hug, pastor."

Helen loved to bake. She baked delicious cookies and often walked over to the church with them to share during our morning coffee break. She told me she often burnt herself and, at least once a day, broke down and cried. But she didn't let her frustration stop her. She stopped going to the support group for the blind, because she got tired of hearing the others complain, gripe and feel sorry for themselves!

I tell you about Helen because Helen had a choice. She could have chosen to feel sorry for herself, roll herself up into the fetal position, whine and shrivel up to die. Instead, she chose to answer God's call to ministry with children. How she loved children! They knew she loved them, and they loved her. She was a woman with a mission, undeterred. Helen's thorn was her loss of sight, but she discovered and trusted God's "sufficient grace."

Martha

Martha was stone deaf and could only communicate one-on-one. I asked her if she heard anything at the worship services. She said, "No, not even the organ or the choir." As she rarely missed a Sunday, I asked her why she came. She drew herself up and snorted, "I want everyone to know whose side I'm on!"

My thorn?

Two specialists told me that I was developing chronic laryngitis, which would make it impossible to preach, teach and sing! Sinusitis was the culprit caused by cold and windy weather. Eventually the "thorn" sent us to California but first to St. Louis Park, where Craig was born. Aldersgate Church is located in St. Louis Park, a suburb of Minneapolis.

Eighteen months previously in February, we spent a week in Florida, a Christmas gift from Ellie's father. We left Tampa at 80 degrees and flew non-stop to Minneapolis, where we landed at 20 degrees below zero, a drop of 100 degrees in a few hours. My sore throat from sinus infection did not clear until October!

Concerned about chronic laryngitis, I asked the District Superintendent if I might transfer to a warmer climate. He suggested that doing educational ministry in a city church, without driving in the country and constantly going in and out of drafty buildings, might help me with my sinus condition. And so, I went to Aldersgate as Minister of Education.

Aldersgate

Developing a strong weekend retreat and week-long summer camp ministry for children and youth was a challenge and a joy. The church purchased a used school bus, and I was the driver.

The church also had a large three-year confirmation program. 150 junior high students (grades 7, 8 and 9) met

37

Wednesday afternoons, a horrible time of day. Discipline was not easily enforced. At one Official Board meeting, I moved that we give up the 8th grade for Lent!

The senior high youth group met on Sunday evenings. A mother told me how much her son enjoyed the group. Astonished, I replied, "He has never come!" Evidently, she dropped him off and picked him up. Who knows where he went. But, according to him, he enjoyed the group.

Aldersgate had a Dixieland jazz band composed of church members (all men, at that time), and I had fun joining them and playing the piano.

When the sinus condition did not improve, with frequent attacks continuing, I began investigating the possibility of moving to a warmer climate. I met with a District Superintendent in Albuquerque and a United Church of Christ Conference Minister in Southern California in late 1968.

CHAPTER SEVEN

California, Here We Come!

During a reception for the retiring Minneapolis District Superintendent one Sunday in June, Dennis Nyberg asked me to go with him to the First United Methodist Church of Palo Alto, California, as one of his Associates. Then he approached Ellie, who was serving coffee, and asked her if she had ever been to California. When we got in the car, I told her what Dennis had asked. She immediately responded, "You're going, aren't you."

Dennis had long been pastor of Lake Harriet Church and was respected throughout the denomination for his social justice leadership. When he was asked to go to Palo Alto, he received permission to recruit a Minister of Education. He researched and chose me.

We became very good friends with Dennis and Kaye, and we kept in touch through the years. They were "grandparents" to our boys. After Dennis retired, they moved back to Minnesota. Dennis happened to be visiting us in Arizona the day our twin granddaughters were born. We visited the Nybergs whenever we returned to Minnesota to visit family. Kaye died in 2000. Our last visit with Dennis in his Minnesota home was four days after his 93rd birthday. He died a few months later.

Dennis asked me to be his Associate in June; in July we were flown to Palo Alto for the interview. While there, we also rented a townhouse for our September arrival. Our furniture left in August, and we drove across country, pulling our travel trailer.

* * *

When we left Salt Lake City and drove across the salt desert and Nevada's barren terrain, our mouths opened in awe as we shook our heads at scenery far different from green Minnesota with its 10,000 lakes. When we drove through Winnemucca, we noticed the United Methodist Church across the street from a casino. I told the family, "This church is in the Conference. I might be appointed here someday!" We almost turned around and went back home!

Palo Alto

First United Methodist Church is located in downtown Palo Alto, the home of Stanford University. The present sanctuary was built in 1963, a magnificent structure that resembles the Air Force chapel in Colorado Springs.

I was in charge of the education ministry—children, youth and adults. In the summer, I directed several camps. During one of the camps, an eight-year old girl came up to me, crying. I asked, "What happened?" She replied, "Johnny swore at me with his finger!" I told her to look the other way.

The youth ministry featured weekend retreats, summer camps and week-long work camps, which were held during Easter vacation. The teenagers painted two church buildings, painted dormitories at Cesar Chavez's headquarters near Bakersfield, where they also learned first-hand about the Farm Worker Movement and painted the corral for the Heifer Project near Modesto.

The doorbell rang at an ungodly, early hour, long before the school day began. I was still in my pajamas. Two girls from the senior high youth group greeted me with, "Happy birthday! You're being kidnapped!" After I dressed, they proceeded to blindfold me, put me in the back seat and drive. Eventually we started to climb a curvy road. It was hot in the back seat beneath the blindfold. I tried to control myself, but finally said, "Please pull over and stop." They did. I stumbled out and proceeded to throw up. They didn't know how easily I get carsick! How embarrassed I was! How sorry they were! They took off the blindfold, and we drove to Foothill Park where the rest of the group was waiting by picnic tables laden with breakfast.

Housing

The church had at one time owned three parsonages in Palo Alto, but in its wisdom (?) had sold them by the time Dennis and I arrived on the scene. When we came, the cost of houses in Palo Alto was beyond our reach. After four months in a rented townhouse, we purchased a home in Sunnyvale, 16 miles from the church.

The 20-minute commute was manageable, but five years later the traffic had increased and often it took 45 minutes to get home for dinner, which was a re-fueling stop before returning for evening meetings.

When I returned to Palo Alto nine years later as Senior Pastor, church members helped us purchase a home in Palo Alto. Ten years later when we moved, the church purchased our share and Palo Alto Church again had a parsonage.

CHAPTER EIGHT

Go . . . Out of the World!

Camps and retreats are very important ministries where children, youth and adults come "out" of their everyday worlds, away from school, workplace, home, family and familiar environments to "get away from it all" in a fun, comfortable, secure setting where Christian friendships are found, the Bible is studied and the love of God is experienced.

Minnesota camping

"The car's missing!" shrieked Ellie. We were on a camping trip with the Milaca Church youth, and she had gone to the Volkswagen bug in the morning to get baby supplies. We started searching. No kids or adult counselors offered to help. Eventually, we found the car in a tent where they had carried it! Oh, how they laughed!

Canoe trips with youth into the northern Minnesota boundary waters were fun and challenging. Portaging between lakes carrying back packs with clothing, food, cooking equipment, and canoes was no small task. On my first trip, I left home with the flu. The doctor gave me antibiotics and assured me I would be fine. The leaders put me in the middle of a canoe and I thoroughly enjoyed the ride, majestic scenery and drinking the clean lake water. On the next trips, there was no free ride!

When I was transferred to Aldersgate Church in St. Louis Park, I continued the canoe trips. On one trip a young man appeared carrying a reel-to-reel portable record player. At the orientation meeting, I explained that there was no radio reception in the wilderness area, so there he came with his own music. I imagined the ruining of the wilderness peace with his loud music, but on the first portage he dropped it in the water and it never did work.

Family Camp

"We need a Director." The voice on the phone sounded panicked! It was the District Director of Camping, a neighboring pastor in Saratoga, California. "In just a few weeks, our annual Family Camp (since 1957) will be held, and we have no director." I sang, *"I'll go if you want me to go, dear Lord."* I already was directing several summer camps for Palo Alto children and youth, but this would be an opportunity for our family to go to camp together.

That was in 1971, and I'm still the director as of this writing. Marylee Sheffer, now a pastor and a Family Camper since her marriage, was added as co-director several years ago, for which I am thankful. Her children, and husband Ralph (who as a child had begun coming to camp in the 1950s), are active family campers.

White Sulphur Springs

There were 28 of us that first year, now there are 250. The pungent aroma of sulphur, like rotten eggs, greeted us when we arrived at White Sulphur Springs in the Napa wine country, near St. Helena. The buildings were old but adequate. Each family had its own cabin, and meals were served in the dining hall. The feature of the camp was the sulphur spring hot tub, which accommodated about 12 people. Oh, the stench! But what fun we had.

The drawback to the campground was the county road that ran through the middle. There was not much traffic, but watching children was a constant necessity. The Conference sold the campground in 1973.

Lodestar

In 1974, we went to Camp Lodestar near Wilseyville, but a fire several months later destroyed the dining hall/meeting room. The camp featured an outdoor amphitheater with a stage. The hilarious skit "Mother, I Am Wounded" originated here, and through the years it has been updated and often repeated, much to everyone's delight.

Years later when I was chairperson of the Conference Camping Committee and then chairperson of the Board of Discipleship, I suggested that the Conference needed a campground in the Sierras to complement Monte Toyon Camp which is located near the ocean in Aptos. When Camp Lodestar became available, the Conference purchased it.

Silver Spur

Since 1975, Family Camp has been held at Silver Spur, near Tuolumne in the Sierras. Silver Spur has become our home. Each family has either its own room in the lodge or its own cabin. Single persons share. Our camp is usually held the third week of June.

Through the years, our campers have given funds to initiate and help build a tennis court, children's play yard, outdoor lounge area and a sidewalk to the amphitheater. In 2010, we raised $17,000 to encourage the enlargement of the dining hall. Silver Spur now plans to build a new dining hall and kitchen. We have also raised funds for hurricane and Midwest tornado relief. For several years, quilts were made for Paul Newman's Painted Turtle Camp for seriously ill children. A quilt is usually raffled each year to raise money for camperships.

Camp Activities

A multitude of varied activities for the week are printed on the daily schedule. Music from our camp guitar band fills the morning air calling us together for the 9:00 meeting with singing from our own songs books and a Bible story in the outdoor amphitheater, followed by age-level classes.

Activities offered from which campers can choose and plan their day include:

children's swimming classes, swimming, water aerobics, softball and volleyball teams, arts, crafts and tie dying, quilting, archery, climb the wall, giant swing, tennis, water slide, zipline, singing lessons, brass/woodwind band, Name That Tune, line dancing/U-Jam/Just Dance, tai-chi, children's Olympic games, children's story time during Flake Out, jigsaw puzzles, visiting, resting or reading in

Shady Rest, water rockets, and yo-yo performance and lessons.

Preschool child care is provided every morning for two hours to give parents a break.

The sports are child friendly. In volleyball, a child can serve close to the net and gets three tries; in softball, there are no strikeouts and a child under the age of 10 is assured first base.

We have so much fun entertaining each other that we have two evenings of Talent Night. Performing in front of people who love you provides children and youth with priceless experience in public speaking—gaining confidence, self-esteem and stage presence.

Younger children, older children, younger youth and older youth each lead an evening campfire with skits, singing and prayer. The closing campfire is a Communion service.

Curfew for children ages 12 and under is at 10:00. Youth and adult curfew is at 1:00. Table games are popular after the children go to bed. Rummikub is a favorite of the older crowd; younger couples play a variety of games and visit.

Here comes the bride

It might be a first for a camp, but we have had a wedding! Mark and Kim met at camp and were married in the outdoor amphitheater with the reception in the dining hall. I proudly officiated. It was a hot day, but a grand celebration—an inspiring, unforgettable event.

We also had another first. During Talent Night instead of singing the song that was on the program, Laura invited her sister Michelle to the stage. Craig began playing the electric piano and Tim, wearing a black tuxedo coat, white shirt, black bow tie, short pants, sandals, and carrying one rose, walked down the center aisle. He handed the rose to Michelle, sang a solo, got on his knees, pulled out a ring and said into the microphone, "Michelle, will you marry me?" She screamed "Yes!", and the weeping camp exploded with a standing ovation!

Several other married couples met at camp, including our youngest son Craig and Laura. Brian proposed to Marjorie at camp, and then announced her acceptance.

Who comes to Family Camp?

Several multi-generational families attend every year. When children are grown, marry and have their children, they all come. Many singles also participate, so the term Family Camp is expanded to include married and singles. Truly, we all belong to a larger family.

Our oldest camper was Isobel who came every year until she reached 101! Her favorite activity was playing Rummikub until the 1:00am curfew. Lolita came until she was no longer able. She died at the age of 105. The youngest camper was Kami, one-week old.

Phil

An inspiring camper was Phillip Bennett, an amazing teenager, who came to camp for several years in his wheelchair. It was difficult understanding him because of

48

his disability. Phil endured Friedreich's Ataxia, a horrible disease—an inherited, progressive genetic neuromuscular disorder; in shorthand: the inability to coordinate muscle movements.

Yet Phil refused to be controlled by his condition. He hung out with the teenagers, even dancing in skits with his wheelchair. His mantra, the theme of his life, was: "All we have to decide is what to do with the time that is given to us." His courage and persistence are captured in his compelling autobiography, *Living the Decision* (available on Amazon.com).

Phil positively lived his life to the fullest—sometimes angry, sometimes frustrated, but never giving up. He wrote, "As bad as it was, there was a bright side. There's always a bright side. But, sometimes it's barely a shade brighter than pitch black."

But persist he did, with adventure and risk. Phil rappelled—plunged into the depths of Moaning Caverns, trusting the rope. He loved Great America, especially going to the head of the lines in his wheelchair! His favorite ride was the roller coaster ride, Top Gun. Phil's enthusiastic pursuits included skiing, swimming, water skiing, white water rafting, sky diving, shot put, discus throwing, riding on airplanes by himself, and a trip to New York City with a helpmate.

Philip took on a mission to raise funds for Ataxia research and raised over $250,000. Proceeds from the sale of his book continue to fund the research.

What Family Camp has become

Our camp has developed traditions through the years—family photos, t-shirts with our camp logos, reunions, annual poem and a website—familycamp.org.

Family Camp has become an extended family for many, including ours as most of our relatives live in Minnesota. Our children saw their grandparents only a few times a year, but have had Family Camp grandparents, aunts, uncles and cousins throughout the years.

United Methodist pastors are frequently moved from church to church, preventing the fostering of long-term relationships. What a joy it has been for me to participate in Family Camp for over 40 years—watching infants become children, youth, young adults; then marry, have children, and proudly bring them to camp!

*   *   *

In her 2007 poem, Judy wrote:

What is Family Camp?

Camp is a little piece of heaven opening its arms,

Welcoming us, renewing us with its charms.

We are filled with God's overwhelming grace,

As we see God's love on each other's face.

This is a place to celebrate and rejoice

A place to give thanks and lift voice.

Here we are accepted as we are—

Tall, short, young, old, each one a star.

*   *   *

Betsy wrote in July 2012, "I don't think that there is another community anywhere in the world like our Family Camp Community and I am honored to be a part of this big loving family."

*   *   *

It is amazing how one week a year affects our campers. The relationships established and nourished, and the blessings received from God are astounding.

CHAPTER NINE

How to Know the Will of God

Jesus struggled to do the will of God. In the Garden of Gethsemane the night before his execution, Jesus agonized over his future but, ultimately, completely submitted himself to the will of God. It is not easy to do the will of God. It is not easy to do that for which you were born. The path ahead is not necessarily paved, level and clear. It is marred with potholes, loaded with detours and bordered by treacherous cliffs.

Why were you born? Why are you here upon the earth at this time? Many people never ask this question of themselves, or if they do ask it, they find no answer. The famous psychiatrist Carl Jung has said, "The central neurosis of our time is emptiness." Emptiness, no purpose, no goal, no sense of mission, no assertion of "For this was I born." Yogi Berra of the New York Yankees said, "If you don't know where you're going, you're likely to end up someplace else!"

*   *   *

General William Booth saw poverty, and he gave his life to serving the poor. For this was he born. When he was asked, "What is the secret of your success?" Booth answered, "I will tell you the secret. There have been many people with far greater abilities, far greater opportunities, but my secret is that God has had all there was of me to have." General Booth saw a need, judged that need in accordance with what is right and wrong, and totally committed himself to the cause. The Salvation Army was born and history thrust greatness upon Booth.

Why were you born? If you don't know the answer to that question, don't despair. We are not born knowing the reason for our birth. Discovering why you were born is a long process. Few great persons knew in advance what their mission was. In fact, as I read history, greatness is something that was thrust upon them.

The key was in their response. William Booth responded to the cries of poverty. His greatness lay in being at the right place at the right time, with high principles and devotion to what is right, and being willing to commit himself wholeheartedly, totally, to the call of God. John F. Kennedy was asked, "How did you become a war hero?" Kennedy replied, *"It was involuntary. They sunk my boat."* No one decides ahead of time to be a war hero. It depends on the circumstances and, decidedly, it depends upon the response. According to Gore Vidal in his novel *Empire*, Abraham Lincoln once said, *"I do not act. I am acted upon."*

What if these "greats" had chosen otherwise? What if they had chosen not to get involved? What if they had chosen security and financial well-being instead of risking their futures? What if they had let themselves get bitten by the bug of apathy and complacency? William Booth could have visited the slums, decided not to get involved, and gone on with his life. What if these people we call great had chosen otherwise? Who can imagine what the world would be like if these great persons had never realized their greatness?

For what were you born? It's a matter of choice. Every day you are confronted with choices. Will you choose what is easy or what is right? Will you choose what the majority say is right or what your conscience inspired by the Scriptures says is right? Will you choose truth or propaganda? Will you choose what is expedient or will you risk? Will you choose the status quo or what is just? Will you choose conformity or the will of God? As you make your daily choices, you prepare yourself for the big decisions.

For what you were born—finding your mission and purpose in life—is a matter of response to what is thrust upon you. Begin with high principles, a vision of what life might be like, with a high priority on truth, and a deep conviction of what is right and what is just. Then, be open to the possibilities and challenges which confront you, often daily. Through prayer and study, be open to the Holy Spirit. Finally, add commitment—your willingness to give yourself totally, without reservation. Give God all of you there is to have, and you will discover your destiny. You will gradually come to know the will of God and why you were born.

*   *   *

High principles and a vision of what life might be like begins with the Bible.

1) The Ten Commandments, Exodus 20:1-17:

You shall have no other gods before me.

You shall not make for yourself an idol.

You shall not make wrongful use of the name of the Lord your God.

Remember the Sabbath day and keep it holy.

Honor your father and your mother.

You shall not murder.

You shall not commit adultery.

You shall not steal.

You shall not bear false witness against your neighbor.

You shall not covet.

2) Jesus said the greatest commandment is, Mark 12:30-31, "You shall love the Lord your God" (which summarizes the first four commandments) and "You shall love your neighbor as yourself" (which summarizes the last six commandments). Expanding on "love your neighbor," Jesus said, Luke 6:31, "Do to others as you would have them do to you."

3) Micah 6:8, "And what does the Lord require of you but to do justice, and to love kindness, and to walk humbly with your God."

In the novel, *St. Francis*, by Nikos Kazantzakis, Francis and Brother Leo are walking. Francis speaks,

"Brother Leo, the only joy in this world is to do God's will . . ."

". . . But, Brother Francis, sometimes we want many things. Which among all of them is the will of God?"

"The most difficult," Francis answered with a sigh.

In my first churches, I was a brash young college student eager to serve but not fully aware of what I was getting myself into. I soon learned that following the will of God led me into difficult situations where I learned to trust in God.

My first funeral

The first funeral I conducted by myself is a vivid memory. An active, bouncy, attractive, darling red headed girl became gravely ill. I don't recall what her illness was, but she was sent to the University of Minnesota Hospital. I visited her in the ICU where she was hooked up to many tubes. Her mother had remarried by that time and going to her husband's church in another town. When we planned the funeral, I asked her mother to invite her new pastor to participate in the service.

The church was packed for the funeral. A few minutes before the service started, I stood on the church steps waiting for the pastor to appear. When he did, I thanked him for coming, and asked him if he would like to read the Scripture lesson. He gruffly said, "No" and walked by without a greeting or a hand shake. I stood there numb. The mortician put his hand on my shoulder and said, "Don't let him bother you. They from that denomination are all that way!" The mortician comforted me!

CHAPTER TEN

"Difficult" Challenges

I don't know how it happened, but singing "I'll go where you want me to go, dear Lord" and following the will of God's most difficult path led me into several crisis situations where I was given the task of crisis management and healing.

"We have a crisis"

The District Superintendent called. It was 1983, and I was asked to return to the First United Methodist Church of Palo Alto as Senior Pastor. Ironically, my first Sunday was also Recycling Sunday!

It had been four years since the crisis; but rebuilding is a long, slow process, and the church was still reeling. One-half of the congregation had left the church.

Craig was entering the junior year of high school, and transferring to a new school for his final two years was not an easy decision. Ellie and I talked it over with him, and he magnanimously agreed to go. Having friends from Family Camp at Palo Alto High School was a plus.

I stayed ten years in Palo Alto, which at that time was the church's longest pastorate since R. Marvin Stuart left in 1964 and became a bishop. He was pastor for 22 years during which time the church's membership grew to become the largest in the conference. A magnificent "cathedral"similar in architecture to the Air Force Academy Chapel in Colorado was erected on the original site.

The attendance and membership grew while I was there, but not to its former glory.

I was senior pastor of the Palo Alto Church for ten years. Adding in the previous five years when I was an associate pastor, a grand total of 15 years was spent in Palo Alto—unforgettable, productive, fulfilling and challenging years. On January 23, 2006 I was honored as Senior Pastor Emeritus with the presentation of a beautiful plaque during the worship service.

"We have a crisis . . ."

(Again!) It was 1993. The District Superintendent explained that the Merced Church was in crisis. I sang, *"I'll go where you want me to go, dear Lord."* Merced, called the Gateway to Yosemite, is the county seat of Merced County, in the central valley. The famous Merced River flows through Yosemite Park, past Merced and joins the Stanislaus River.

The pastor had been removed by the Bishop. The congregation was incensed and didn't believe the accusations. The pastor and family moved out of the parsonage just before Christmas, and an interim pastor was appointed until July when I arrived. The congregation stopped paying conference appointments and used the money to pay his salary until June when he returned to New England where he was appointed to a church.

The congregation reacted negatively to how the District Superintendent handled the situation. When she announced that the pastor was removed and she would conduct the Sunday services, she was told, "No way! We will get an injunction to keep you off the property."

A few Sundays later, the Bishop preached. The choir sang Jim Strathdee's anthem, and repeated several times the phrase, "*Let justice flow down like a mighty river.*" Following the service, 300 people gathered in Fellowship Hall. After a short presentation, the Bishop expected to divide the group into small groups for "counseling," led by invited leaders. But someone asked, "Bishop, are you going to change your mind?" When the Bishop said, "No," 300 people, without prior planning, spontaneously got up and walked out, leaving the Bishop and the "counselors" by themselves.

Because of the strong feelings toward the Superintendent, the Bishop asked the Nevada District Superintendent to meet with the church's Staff-Parish Relations Committee and arrange for a new pastor. In the meantime, the interim pastor, John Moore, did an outstanding job beginning the healing process.

When Ellie and I arrived in July, we had a guest, Ian, from Australia with us. He helped us move, and we took him on a tour of Merced, completely forgetting my first meeting with the Staff-Parish Relations Committee! On Sunday, I confessed to the congregation and told them that probably the next pastor was already waiting in the wings. But they embraced Ellie and me, and we had an unforgettable, happy ministry in Merced.

In the Fall, the church held its annual meeting. The Nevada District Superintendent conducted the church conference. When it was time for the pastor's report, I said, "I understand why you are not paying the conference apportionments. I realize you are angry with the Bishop and Superintendent. However, by not paying the pension portion of the apportionments, you are not hurting the Bishop, you are hurting (and I named two widows of former pastors who were receiving pension payments)." Immediately Lillian spoke up, "I move we pay the pension portion of the apportionments!"

In February, the Bishop asked me to schedule a meeting for the purpose of reconciliation. There were about 12 people at the meeting representing committees of the church. I asked them to share their concerns. After they had expressed their anger, hurt feelings and disappointment, the Bishop shared how he also felt disappointment and even betrayal. "Because," he said, "the Staff-Parish Relations Committee broke confidentiality by informing the congregation what was transpiring." Incredibly, the chair of the SPRC denied the blame. "We didn't break the confidentiality. We did not spread the word; the pastor did. He returned from his meeting with you and began telling folks he had been wronged." The tension in the room relaxed as the Bishop relaxed.

I then asked the Bishop what he meant by reconciliation; what needed to happen? He replied that he wanted the church to reconcile with the District Superintendent. The room erupted! Several shared why they were upset with her. The Bishop's eyes grew larger and larger. I can't say there was a correlation, but the next week all clergy in the conference received a letter from the Bishop informing them that the District Superintendent would be returning to the pastorate and a new Superintendent would begin July 1.

Merced Church members proved to be resilient, faithful to God and committed to the future, and Merced became a happy, thriving church.

My shortest appointment

My longest appointment as a United Methodist pastor lasted for ten years (fifteen when you add my appointment as Associate Pastor) as Senior Pastor of the First United Methodist Church of Palo Alto.

My shortest appointment? 24 hours!

The Bishop called this time. "We have a crisis." Here I go again, singing "I'll go where you want me to go, dear Lord . . ."

On Tuesday, August 15, 2000, at 10:00 AM, I arrived at the Fresno District office to meet with the Fresno District Superintendent, the Delta District Superintendent and the Conference Treasurer.

The District Superintendent explained that she was suspending the Pastor of St. Luke's United Methodist Church, Fresno, and appointing me as the interim pastor.

The Pastor was the sixth evangelical United Methodist pastor to oppose the conference's liberal policies on homosexuality. He had already organized and incorporated a new, independent St. Luke's Community Church and was taking offerings for the new congregation; a box for contributions was in the narthex. Also, the Superintendent had recently learned that in May St. Luke's United Methodist Church had been mortgaged for $130,000 without the authorization of the District Superintendent as required by The United Methodist Book of Discipline.

We drove to St. Luke's. The Superintendent asked to see the Pastor and was informed that he was out of town. She then asked to speak to the Office Manager, informed her that she was suspending the Pastor and introduced me as the interim pastor. The Office Manager gulped and shook my hand.

I asked if we might have a staff meeting. The Associate Pastor (who was a United Methodist and a seminary graduate; but had not been ordained or appointed by the Bishop), Youth Pastor, Secretary, Treasurer and Office Manager gathered. I told them I was sorry to be there, it was a sad time; but I hoped they would stay on and keep doing their jobs. A question about the Pastor salary was asked, and the Superintendent answered that a pastor on suspension can receive full salary for up to 60 days. The

Office Manager then said the staff would like to meet alone.

After they adjourned, I asked the Office Manager if the staff had agreed to stay. "Yes," she replied and asked me what I needed. Explaining that I did not feel comfortable sitting in the Pastor's office, I asked her where I might have a space. She suggested the library. I asked for and received the Membership Directory, Administrative Directory, finance statement, copies of the latest bank statement and a master key. The staff members were polite, cordial and cooperative.

After lunch, the Superintendent and I went to the district office (three blocks away). She wrote a letter on Fresno District letterhead to be mailed to the congregation announcing the change. I returned to St. Luke's, wrote a letter to accompany hers and asked the Office Manager if they could be mailed the next day. She said she would try, but Wednesday was a busy day preparing the Sunday bulletin.

On my way to the library, I introduced myself to a man pacing the hallway. Evidently he had been called during the lunch break. He was polite, but informed me that I was in hostile territory, that I would not be their pastor and that they resented the takeover.

"Takeover? The Pastor has organized a new church."

"I have been a member here for 35 years. We built these buildings, and they are ours." Later, I checked the Administrative Directory and discovered he was the chair of the Finance Committee.

I also introduced myself to a woman who informed me she was the Director of the Vacation Bible School, which was meeting each evening that week with 200 children. She invited me to supper at 5:30. I asked her if there was an assembly where I could introduce myself to the children. The Finance Chair descended upon us and said, "You are not going there as the Senior Pastor. You are not going to disturb the children." The Director then asked me not to speak. I replied, "You are right. Let's not disturb Bible School and confuse the children." Later, she apologized, and I said, "Don't worry; I just won't come at all."

As the Associate Pastor was teaching a Bible class, I talked to the Youth Pastor, who was also the leader of the Praise Band, about the Sunday service. When the class was over, I asked the Associate Pastor if I might speak with him. He excused himself saying the leaders were going to get ready for Bible School. I asked, "How about tomorrow morning?" We set a 10:00 appointment.

I then went home to Merced to care for Ellie who, because of foot surgeries, was confined to bed and the couch. Thanks to friends in our Merced church family, she was being cared for. That evening I phoned our son Craig. As he and Laura were planning to spend the weekend with us, I asked him if they would accompany me to St. Luke's in case no musicians appeared. Craig is a Stanford trained organist and an accomplished pianist.

Wednesday morning, August 16 (our 42nd wedding anniversary!), I arrived at St. Luke's at 10:20 (I got lost!). The parking lot was empty except for the church van and a van with "Sierra Lock" painted on its side. I laughed and said to myself, "Here we go!"

I went to the office door to discover a business card tucked behind the glass with the message, "Rev. Norris, please call me." As the door was locked, I couldn't turn the card over to see whose it was. I assumed it was the Associate Pastor with whom I had made the appointment. (Later I learned from the *Fresno Bee* the card was from the church's lawyer). When I phoned the pastor's number, his son answered and said his Dad was not there, so I called the Office Manager and asked, "What's going on?"

She replied, "I'm not the one to tell you."

"Who is?"

"The Finance Chair and the Lay Leader are planning to be there to talk to you."

"There's no one here."

"We are not accepting you as our pastor. We already have a pastor, and we are not letting you in the building."

I told her I would go over to the District office because it was too hot to sit in the car.

She thought that was a good idea.

"How are you doing with all this?" I asked her.

"I'm fine. Thank you."

*   *   *

At the District Office I reported to the Superintendent, "I've just had the shortest appointment in history!" She then called the Conference Treasurer who in turn called the

Conference attorney who later advised the Superintendent and me not to go near the building.

The Superintendent called the Bishop who said he had learned that the St. Luke's Trustees had leased the facilities to the new congregation, which they can do legally for 364 days according to the United Methodist Book of Discipline. After that time, the District Superintendent must sign any extension.

The Superintendent had previously scheduled a meeting in Merced with a group of pastors including St. Luke's pastor. I stopped at the church, waited until the meeting was over, walked up to the Pastor, handed him the key and said, "I may as well give this back to you as it doesn't fit anything any more." Confused, he didn't recognize me until I introduced myself. I then informed him that contrary to the Breaking News article on St. Luke's website (which the district secretary had accessed), I had never been pastor of a Reconciling Congregation. He apologized and said that he had me confused with someone else.

"I want to commend you for your staff. They were very polite and cooperative. You have a gifted staff, a vital ministry, a great church! It's a shame that you are putting them through this turmoil."

"Surely you don't mean me personally," and he began to blame the Conference, but I interrupted and said, "You are the one who chose to do this."

*   *   *

And that was my shortest appointment as a United Methodist pastor: 24 hours!

Incidentally, the Superintendent's letter and my letter did not get mailed!

And, no, I was not paid for the 24 hours; not even mileage!

Subsequently, the conference filed a lawsuit against the church. Under United Methodist law, a church building and site are not owned by the congregation, but by the denomination. The church trustees hold the property in trust for the denomination. I was deposed and also testified in court. The judge upheld the conference suit, but the church trustees appealed. On grounds that the Trust Clause in the United Methodist Discipline is ambiguous, and can be interpreted as revocable, rather than irrevocable, the California Appeals Court overturned the previous decision.

St. Luke's Community Church is now meeting in the former St. Luke's United Methodist Church building. Ironically one of the first actions of the new congregation was to fire the Pastor!

I'll go . . . to Paradise!

"We need your gifts and graces." Arizona Bishop Bill Dew, who had been my District Superintendent in California, phoned this time. The Senior Pastor of Paradise Valley United Methodist Church in suburban Phoenix was leaving the end of December 2000, and an Interim Senior Pastor was needed for six months, which actually turned into eight months. The church was in turmoil.

The popular pastor and gifted preacher had left abruptly, leaving many questions, apprehensions and grief in his wake. I struggled about my first Sunday and decided to take a risk.

Before saying a word in each of the three morning services, I sang the song, *"I don't know what you came to do, but I came to praise the Lord"* interspersing spoken questions:

Did you come to judge?

Did you come to criticize?

Did you come to check out the new guy?

Did you come because your mother made you come?

Did you come because it is the right thing to do?

Well, *"I don't know what you came to do, but I came to praise the Lord,"* and ended the song by inviting the congregation to join in singing and clapping. It went over big!

It was a privilege to lead our six clergy staff (two were part-time), a Director of Christian Education, and several lay program staff. The eight months were positive and productive.

I'll go . . . to Mission Bell

In October 2003, the phone rang in our California home, "This is the District Superintendent of the Phoenix West District. We have a distraught congregation and need an interim pastor for eight months, beginning immediately. The beloved pastor of Mission Bell is leaving to go on staff at a mega Lutheran Church." (Ironically, a few years later she returned to pastor a United Methodist Church.)

We packed our bags, got on the road and for eight months, commuting one hour each way from our home in Gilbert, had another delightful, productive interim ministry

Do you know the way to San Jose?

As I was hauling a van load of "stuff" from our Gilbert house to our new house in Mesa, in May 2007, the northern California Bishop called on my cellphone. "We would like you to serve as Interim Senior Pastor at our Wesley Church for six months."

When I reached the new house, I gathered our moving task force together—Ellie, son Tim, his cousin-in-law, and Elaine, our son Craig's mother-in-law who had flown from Stockton to help us move. They rationalized. "After all, it's only six months." Singing, *"I'll go where you want me to go,"* little did I know that the six months would turn into eighteen!

Wesley Church, the flag-ship Japanese American church in the Conference, is located in San Jose's Japantown. Because of my experience in Japan, I was asked to be the Interim Senior Pastor.

I was replacing Mariellen as Senior Pastor of Wesley when she became the Fresno District Superintendent. As the Bishop felt it was important to find a person of Japanese ancestry to be the senior pastor, I was asked to be the interim pastor in the meantime. Originally the process was to be completed in six months, but it took 18 months to do so! I became the first Caucasian pastor since the church was organized in 1895.

On my first Sunday, I told the congregation about my Nagoya experience and of how I first met Mariellen when she came to California. I asked her if she had been born in Nagoya, Japan. She affirmed it and also that her parents were Ben and Lily. I exclaimed, "I used to hold you and burp you!" She quickly replied, "I hope I threw up on you!" Oh, how the congregation laughed at the story, and several said, "That sounds like Mariellen."

Over 95% of Wesley's congregation was of Japanese ancestry, although only a few spoke Japanese. For the first-generation Japanese immigrants, Michi, a pastor from Japan, conducted worship services and Bible studies in Japanese. Motoe was the third pastor on staff. She was also from Japan, but spoke English and ministered with the English speaking congregation. She has since been appointed to her own church, the Japanese American church in Sacramento.

The internment

As I was the first Caucasian pastor, Mariellen asked several in the congregation to introduce me to the elderly and shut-ins who lived in their homes or skilled nursing facilities, just in case they were confused to be visited by a tall "gaijin."

I often asked them, "Tell me your story" and then learned about the internment camps during World War II, a record of shame in American history. Ripped from their homes, carrying possessions in suit cases, they were taken and imprisoned, some temporarily in stables at horse racing tracks before being transferred to their permanent camp. Some lost everything; others had Caucasian neighbors or business partners who looked after their property. Even then, burglars often looted. The new Japanese Museum located across the street from Wesley Church has many exhibits of those dark days, including a replica of a typical camp housing unit.

Many of those who had grown up in Hawaii were spared the humiliation of internment. There was an initial roundup of Japanese but as there was and is a sizable Japanese population on Hawaii who were indispensable to the agricultural industry, there was no internment. The Hawaiian influence is readily visible in Wesley Church— the ukulele choir and spam dishes at the potlucks!

The church building played a role in World War II. Then named the Japanese Methodist Church of San Jose, the building became a storehouse for possessions of folks destined for the camps. The Caucasian church down the street—First Methodist—took the cross and communion altarware and stored them in their building.

Differences

The Couples' Club invited us to a luncheon meeting and asked me to speak about how Wesley Church differed from churches I previously served. My first point was, "You all wear black clothes to memorial/funeral services!" And there I was; I didn't even own a black suit. I shared how I was impressed with the strong bond of fellowship that also includes non-Japanese members. While I was pastor, several persons of non-Japanese ancestry joined the church.

And a major difference, I told them, was their potlucks, bounteous with Japanese food! They have many as they enjoy the fellowship. The potlucks are an important part of the ministry as Wesley Church is not a neighborhood church. The members drive long distances, and many see each other only on Sundays. Hence, the importance of potlucks!

A church ukulele choir—20 strummers plus a guitar—was a first for me. Wesley Church also has a Jazz Band. The band not only plays for church functions, but Japantown celebrations, Buddhist Church dances, senior residences, etc.

I ended the talk by saying, "If I had known how special Japanese churches are, I would have asked for an appointment years ago!"

*   *   *

What an unforgettable experience we enjoyed at Wesley Church! Polite, happy, generous, spirit-filled folks quickly became friends.

CHAPTER ELEVEN

Strategies for Crisis Ministry

Finding myself in difficult crisis situations, I learned to trust in God and develop effective strategies.

1) I like it here

Every church was a happy, challenging, experience, and I soon learned that my being happy and enthusiastic was a tremendous advantage. Parishioners soon pick up the pastor's attitude. If one is disappointed to be appointed to that church and is dreaming about the next church; or is homesick for the previous church, the congregation soon learns that they are second choice and the ministry is doomed. For example, one pastor constantly talked about his home sports teams in his sermons but rarely mentioned the teams where he was now living.

However, if the pastor firmly believes and acts as if the Lord has called him/her to be in the present church and wants to be nowhere else, the ministry is off to a flying start. I often called my newsletter column "I Like It Here," borrowing from George Grimm of the Minneapolis Tribune. People responded, "He likes it here, and he likes us!"

2) Find the woman!

I received a thorough, well-rounded, practical education at Garrett Seminary. In the Church Administration class taught by Professor Al Lindgren, a former pastor and district superintendent, I learned, "The first thing you do when you are appointed to a church is to find the woman who runs it!" (Sometimes, but not very often, the woman is a man!)

It was easy to find the women who ran the three country churches, but more difficult in the Milaca Church. I had been there a few months when I walked into the vestibule and saw one of our members painting. The subject had not come up at the Trustees meeting or the Official Board. Surprised, I asked, "Oh, are you going to paint the basement also? It needs it." He said, "I don't know. I'll have to ask Mrs. Jacobsen." I found her! And, thank God, she was a lovely woman, cooperative and totally committed to the church. When building the education building was proposed, she strongly supported it.

3) Get 'em together!

In 2 Corinthians 5:18, Paul wrote that we are given *"the ministry of reconciliation"*—reconciliation with God and reconciliation with one another. But when facing dissension, disagreements, and hurt feelings, what is the most effective way of achieving reconciliation? Face them squarely—head on.

Soon after I began my ministry in Manteca St. Paul's, I was told about a tense situation, complete with hurt feelings. When the new building opened for use a year before I arrived, the United Methodist Women began meeting in the Fireside Room, and took with them the cross and candles that had been used as a worship center in the room where the fourth grade Sunday School class also met. For over a year, there was a stand-off between the women and George, the Sunday School teacher. I said, "Get them together." I invited four women (including the "woman who ran the church!") and the lone Sunday School teacher. I began the meeting by asking, "How can we make this work?" Within ten minutes, the women offered to purchase a new cross and candles for the Sunday School class; I went to the office and brought back the Cokesbury catalog; George picked out a set and exclaimed, "I like these better!" All in ten minutes! Yes, when there is conflict, get 'em together!

4) Use the direct approach

A couple who had been very active in the church were very critical and unhappy with my predecessor. In fact, they had started going to the Baptist Church. When I arrived, they returned to our church and expected to resume leadership roles. I went to their home and told them, "I thought you might like to know that folks are saying you are troublemakers—critical, uncooperative and disloyal." The wife immediately demanded to know who I was quoting; I refused. The husband wept. They humbly re-entered the fellowship, were accepted and became active.

Eventually, they became good friends and were very supportive of me and the ministry.

5) Dream big!

Expand the vision has been a major strategy of my ministry—to challenge the churches to stretch and widen their understanding of who they are and what they might be and do in ministry. In Minnesota where I had four churches, and three were under 25 members, I preached, "When Is a Church Small?" A church is not small when it has few members. A church is small when it has a small vision. A major event for the Milaca Church was the addition of a new beautiful Education Building, with five classrooms, fellowship hall, kitchen and a pastor's study. The Minneapolis architect had grown up in our church. His widowed mother was thrilled to enjoy his work. Years later the sanctuary was added with the same design.

In West Bethel Church (one of my college churches) we purchased an electric organ by "selling" each key.

*   *   *

When Kayla and Syd moved to Manteca, I caught the vision of a Music Ministry. Kayla had been the Director of Music in her previous church. At that time, St. Paul's was paying the chancel choir director $75 a month, and the children's choir director $50 a month. There were two choirs, totaling some 45 people. Imagine the Board meetings when I proposed to hire Kayla at $600 a month and gradually increase it to $1,000 a month, with the challenge to develop a music ministry. Such a struggle we had! "We're a small church," they cried. "Where will we get the money?" There was a strong, vocal minority, but the Manteca people are faithful and supportive; they did not become hostile or vindictive in their opposition. They didn't leave the church! They were not small thinking people, but they did resist!

But Kayla and I had a vision. Palo Alto First Church had a strong music ministry so I knew what a music ministry could be. I knew what it would do for the lives of children, youth and adults. I knew that it would not hurt, but enhance the Christian education program. There need be no conflict; in fact, they go hand in hand. When one is weak, they both are weak.

Soon families with children and youth caught the vision. They could see their children in worship and musicals. In no time, Kayla had 37 in two children choirs and 23 in a youth choir.

Next we challenged the congregation to purchase handbells. They shook their heads, "Who needs handbells, and, besides, we have no money." So, we "sold" each handbell by suggesting that a handbell be purchased in memory or in honor of someone special in their lives (different size bells were different prices). Soon we had a four-octave set of handbells, the first handbell choir in Manteca. We also "sold" keys and purchased a Rodgers organ.

In 1½ years, the church had four vocal choirs and two handbell choirs with 120 persons involved. And a youth musical went on the road!

Regarding funds: when expanding ministries, the lack of funds should not considered an obstacle. Of course churches have money; but much of it is still in members' pockets!

Manteca church bought a 15-passenger van for youth trips. In addition, I took senior citizens on field trips. How they loved that! We ran a contest to name the van. Joe, the custodian, won with his suggestion, which was then painted on the side: St. Paul's Care-Van.

*   *   *

After Manteca, I was appointed to First UMC, Modesto, a downtown church in the county seat of Stanislaus County, central California. The building occupies one half of the city block. As with many downtown churches, it had declined over the years, but worship attendance and the children's ministry grew while I was there. In fact, the number of preschool children in Sunday School grew from zero to 25. A Mother's Day fundraiser raised $25,000 for a van and refurbishing projects.

*   *   *

While I was Senior Pastor in Palo Alto, the Centennial Endowment Fund was established. 25 years later in 2013, it totals $ 2,700,000. It is annually funding many special projects and missions, including a 2013 $10,000 grant to the Douglas and Eleanor Norris Scholarship Fund at Garrett-Evangelical Theological Seminary. Also, a preschool and a counseling center were organized and Peggy Goochey, Minister of Program Development developed a Creative Drama Ministry.

*   *   *

While I was pastor in Merced, the church bought a van for the youth. A garage was built to house the van, showers were installed and the patio and children's play area were completely redone. An After School program for the neighboring elementary school was launched.

Challenging others to catch the vision—The Merced Trustees scheduled a Work Day for a Saturday, but, early in the week, it was discovered that most, if not all, of the Trustees would not be able to participate, including the chairperson who was away on a business trip. The logical thing to do was to cancel the Work Day. That was the majority report. But then my wife, Ellie, heard of the cancellation. She said, "We can't do that. It has been announced. People are planning to come. How will they feel if they arrive to work and find out it has been canceled? Besides that, there is work to be done. Classrooms need painting. Outside doors need touchup." She got on the telephone and began recruiting. In the calling, she discovered that, yes, several were planning to come because they had read the announcements. Don, an older retired member, lamented, "I just can't say "No" to that woman!"

Lloyd and Richard stepped forward to be foremen. 45 people were organized into three teams. A team came on Friday and prepared the rooms. Saturday morning a team painted and refinished. Saturday afternoon a team cleaned, including windows and blinds. Several sent in home-made baked goods. The workers had a great time fellowshipping, feasting and working together. And, our children now had bright, fresh classrooms in which to learn about Jesus.

Led by Jody, Merced had a vibrant youth ministry. Kristen Marshall heard the call to ministry and is now an ordained, very successful United Methodist pastor.

*   *   *

I challenged my congregations:

"Some of you may be saying, 'Merced County's economy is in a slump. Interest rates are down. And, you want us to give even more. Are you crazy?'

Of course, I'm crazy. I've staked my life on Jesus. Would you want a pastor who is not crazy? Would you like one that is satisfied with things the way they are? Would you rather be part of a dying church or a *crazy* church?"

*   *   *

While I was pastor of Wesley Church, Soko Hardware decided to sell its adjoining property which also included a parking lot, restaurant, large hall and upstairs rooms. After several brainstorming sessions with the congregation as to how Wesley might use the property, a committee was appointed to negotiate a price. Subsequently, after I left, the property was purchased for $2.4 million with pledges and just a small loan. For years the congregation had been growing the Building Fund.

6) The magic words

Whatever happened to "thank you," "good job," "well done"?

Most of the meals served (not potlucks) to groups inside and outside of the church were prepared by a group of dedicated women. After a sumptuous lunch, I went into the kitchen and thanked them. With tears in her eyes, the woman in charge said, "I can't remember the last time a pastor came into the kitchen!"

When the Church Administrator read the comment I had written after a special project she had completed—"Well done, good job!—she gasped and showed it to a secretary. It had been a long time, she said, since she had been complimented or thanked by the pastor!

During a small group gathering, we were discussing the importance of giving thanks. Lloyd spoke of how he had long wanted to find his favorite elementary school teacher and thank her. He had attended a one-room school in the country and Miss Taylor was his favorite teacher. He especially remembered how she read to them about dinosaurs. Through the years, he had tried to find out what happened to her. Millie, who had lived in the next block for years and was, with Lloyd, an active member of the church, spoke up and said, "Why, I'm Miss Taylor. That was my name at the time. And, yes I read the story about dinosaurs." Lloyd was dumfounded and I don't think he really believed that she was his favorite teacher until she brought a photo of the class to church the next day. Even then, his head was shaking!

Write thank you letters or notes. On Thanksgiving Sunday, I often encouraged the congregation to write a thank you letter to someone who had made a difference in their lives. One Thanksgiving, I wrote a letter to my 5th, 6th and 7th grade teacher (yes, the same one!). She was tough, demanding and strict. We students complained about her at the time, but in later years I realized she was one of the best teachers I had. I wrote and told her so. I hadn't seen her in years when she came to one of our class reunions. Laughing, she told the group how she, a faithful Roman Catholic, reacted with a snort when she received a letter with the return address from a Methodist Church. "Are they trying to convert me?" She reported that she was deeply moved by the letter. How many teachers never know how they have touched lives?

7) Prayer walk

When Jody joined our Merced staff as a Diaconal Minister (later ordained a Deacon), she immediately suggested that we take a Prayer Walk. "What's a Prayer Walk?" I asked. This was a new concept to me. She explained that a Prayer Walk is a walk through church rooms, praying and anointing areas where bad vibes are felt. She gave an example from her former church. On a Prayer Walk, one classroom gave strong vibes. On investigation, she learned that a Boy Scoutmaster had molested boys in that room!

So we did a Prayer Walk. Con, (Jody's husband), Ellie and I joined her as she, with a vial of olive oil, proceeded to walk through the sanctuary, praying and anointing. In the sanctuary, she stopped at two different spots and said, "There is tension here." Amazed, I told her that two antagonistic persons sat in those spots. We prayed for healing. Jody anointed the pews and we continued!

Learning from our Merced experience, when I was appointed to Paradise Valley, Ellie and I went on a Prayer Walk throughout the sanctuary, praying and anointing, "In the name of the Father, Son and Holy Spirit."

CHAPTER TWELVE

"Discharge All the Duties of Your Ministry" (2 Timothy 4:5)

It is a joy and privilege to serve the Lord as a pastor. Doing ministry is an honor. A high point for me is the serving of Holy Communion, calling most by name and offering the body and blood of Christ. Doing ministry is rarely boring and requires flexibility to meet the challenges of events and what is happening in lives.

"I don't know how to read"

"I don't know how to read," a man confessed confidentially when I asked him if he would consider being nominated as chair of the Board of Trustees. Surprised, I wondered how he handled his problem at work. He worked with his hands, and when he needed to read something he was able to finesse and get someone else to do the reading. I told him that we needed him to be chair, and, because I went to all the meetings, I would "protect" him. He accepted the position, and it went well.

Open the windows!

One afternoon I received a phone call. "This is the Manteca Police. We have responded to a marital dispute. They are Methodists, so would you please come?" I didn't know the couple, but I went to their mobile home, praying, "I'll go where you want me to go . . ." The policeman was happy to turn the situation over to me and quickly left.

I entered the home, could barely breathe through the cigarette smoke and could barely see because all the windows were shut and the drapes were closed. My first words were, "Open the windows!" I proceeded to open the drapes and the windows to let in light and air while the couple watched me.

Following his retirement, they had moved to Manteca a few years before. They were Methodists in the Bay Area, but had never been to our church. We talked and I urged them to get out of the house, get to church and do some volunteer work.

They started coming to church, transferred their membership and became very active volunteers.

As far as I know, the police were never called again.

Tennessee Ernie Ford

In October 1991, in the Palo Alto Church sanctuary, I conducted the Memorial Service for Tennessee Ernie Ford, the famous "pea-pickin" country music singer. The previous Easter he introduced himself as "Ernie Ford." I asked him if he was related to Tennessee Ernie Ford. He replied, "I am Tennessee Ernie!" He complimented the choir and especially Leroy's solo in the anthem "Hear Me, Redeemer," written by a local composer, Henry Mollicone. I asked the choir and Leroy to sing it at the Memorial Service. After the service, our Reception Committee hosted a lovely reception. Later I was told by church ushers that Tennessee Ernie through the years would occasionally come to church, arriving after the worship service had started and leaving right after the Benediction. He lived in Portola Valley.

Get your priorities straight!

Doris was elected secretary of the Administrative Council. I called to tell her the first meeting of the year was going to be Sunday evening. She gulped and said that she would be there. I asked her if there was a problem.

"Well, my grandson is competing in a regional gymnastic event in Las Vegas where my oldest daughter lives, and he and his family are going there from their home in Washington."

"So you are planning a mini-family reunion as well as supporting your grandson in the gymnastic event."

"Yes, but I won't go."

You might be interested in my response. "You go to Las Vegas. Your first priority is to be a grandmother."

"Oh, I shouldn't miss the first meeting."

"We can struggle along without you. You go be with your family. Besides that, you can give the church 10% of your winnings!"

"Oh, I don't play those machines!"

Gas or food?

Speaking of priorities, while in college a church in the next town (actually my hometown, St. Francis), sponsored a series of Wednesday evening Sunday School teacher training classes. As I wanted some of our teachers to have the experience, I offered to drive from Hamline University and take them to the class. One of the Wednesdays, I checked my wallet and discovered that I only had money enough either to purchase food until I went home on the weekend or to buy gas to make the round trip. Feeling responsible, and getting my priorities straight, I bought gas and made the trip. When the last woman got out of the car, she handed me a dollar for gas! She had several children and was the least able to afford giving me aid. She said, "I know how hard it is for college students to make it." I feasted on that dollar for two days and learned a lesson on trust and keeping my word!

No turning back

Mary, one of the first women to be ordained in The Methodist Church, was one of the ministers in the Central Minnesota Methodist Parish. It was my privilege to work with her.

Mary's mother lived with her, but when Mary Sr. became ill she wanted to return home to Philadelphia. As Mary's sister had a well-paying career, it was decided that Mary would go and take care of her mother. But, Mary's heart was in ministry to which she had truly been called. Jesus told his disciples to leave their father and their mother, and when you put your hand to the plow, don't turn back. But Mary went to Philadelphia. In ten years, she was dead and her mother was still living.

Versatility required

In each of the three country churches, I was the substitute pianist. When I sang a solo at a funeral I was conducting, the mortician remarked, "I hope you don't take up embalming, too!"

*   *   *

Oh, how it snowed. Milaca is bisected by two state highways, and the snow storm blocked both highways. As the city streets were plowed, I drove to the edge of town and the snow came up to the car's hood! A funeral had been scheduled and the farm family had to travel by snowmobile. The burial was postponed until the snow was removed.

Jesus and His love

Throughout my ministry, I have "told them about Jesus and his love." After a worship service in Palo Alto, a man introduced himself as a Baptist minister from England. He was looking for a Baptist Church, but time had run out and he settled for our church. He told me he was prepared for a liberal sermon, but surprised he said, "If anyone here this morning goes to hell, it won't be your fault!" I took it as a compliment and learned how important it is, regardless of the sermon topic, to include the gospel—to celebrate the love of God and how God is accessible to everyone. I came to realize that whatever the topic, there are lonely, discouraged, grieving, disillusioned, lost persons in the congregation who needed to be told about Jesus.

Barney

Dr. Bernhard W. Anderson, retired biblical professor from Drew University School of Theology and Princeton Theological Seminary, had a sister-in-law in Merced (Lloyd's Miss Taylor) whom he and his wife, Monique, visited fairly often. He appreciated our worship services, and taught a series of classes.

He was the author of several books. I especially appreciate *Understanding the Old Testament.* It was the basic textbook in seminary, and I have used it often through the years.

We had a delightful time together. Barney was a PK (preacher's kid) raised in rural California where he learned to like gospel songs. Several times either at the church or in our home, I played the piano, and he and I sang and sang the old songs—songs that my seminary worship class deemed inappropriate!

CHAPTER THIRTEEN

Turn the Tables—
Don't React, Resist or Fight

Don't use futile tactics that make matters worse, instead . . .

1) Turn the tables

Turning the other cheek, giving your cloak as well as your coat and going the second mile are what I call the Most Misunderstood Teachings. Matthew 5:38-41 begins with Jesus saying, *"Do not resist,"* Why? Because resistance is usually futile. Resisting and attempting to fight a bully who is bigger than you is futile, because you are responding on his terms and using his methods. Jesus said, *"Do not resist,"* and then he proceeded to teach his followers what to do.

Jesus did not say, "Do nothing." We are not to be passive doormats and let people walk all over us. Jesus does not teach us to let people take advantage of us, but to maintain our self-respect and dignity. Jesus expects us to stand up for ourselves and for others. But how we stand up is critical. Rather than resisting, be ingenious, clever, creative, innovative and courageous. Jesus teaches us how by giving examples. Jesus taught strategies on how to turn the tables, take the initiative and keep the initiative.

What did Jesus mean by turning the other cheek, giving your cloak as well as your coat and going the second mile? In order to understand Jesus, we have to understand the culture of Jesus' day. Bible study must begin with the times in which the passage is written. When we look at the environment in which Jesus taught, we discover an entirely different meaning to these teachings.

Turn the other cheek

What does Matthew 5:39 mean, *"If anyone strikes you on the right cheek, turn the other also?"* It is significant that Jesus specified the right cheek. How do you strike someone on the right cheek? Backhand, not by the fist. To strike the right cheek with the fist would require using the left hand. In the Middle East, the left hand is used for unclean tasks. The left hand is never used in eating. The Dead Sea scrolls tell us that even to gesture with the left hand was punished with ten days penance. Therefore, when striking someone, the right hand would be used. And the only way to strike someone on the right cheek is by using the back of the right hand.

What we are dealing with here is not a fistfight but an insult. The intention is to humiliate someone, to put someone in his or her place. A backhand slap was the normal way of reprimanding inferiors. Masters backhanded slaves, husbands backhanded wives, parents backhanded children. You would never backhand a peer, an equal. In fact, there was a stiff penalty for backhanding your equal but no penalty to backhand an inferior.

Therefore, Jesus is teaching his followers what to do when they are backhanded by a so-called superior. You can't resist. You can't hit back. It would be suicidal to hit back using either the right hand or the left! What Jesus cleverly taught was to turn the left cheek to the striker as well. How would he strike the left cheek? He cannot backhand your left cheek with his right hand. Remember, he cannot use his left hand. The only option left is for him to use his fist and hitting you with his fist is to make you his equal! Fistfights are between equals. Backhands are for inferiors. By turning the cheek, the victim is saying to the perpetrator, "I deny you the power to humiliate me. I am a human being. You cannot take away my self-respect." What it means to turn the other cheek is to maintain your dignity. Maintain your self-respect. What the victim did was to take the initiative from the perpetrator, leaving him with no recourse. He was disarmed.

Give your cloak as well

The second example on how to turn the tables, take the initiative and keep the initiative is Mathew 5.40, *"If anyone wants to sue you and take your coat, give your cloak as well."* Usually we understand this to mean generosity. When someone asks you for something, you are to give more than asked. That is not at all what Jesus meant when you understand the circumstances in which Jesus was teaching. Note the word "sue." The system conspired against the common people. Rome taxed heavily in order to finance its army and wars. This forced the gentry to rob poor people of their land, possessions and even their clothes! They did it through the process of lending money. The interest charged was exorbitant. The poor had no choice. They had to borrow. They had to feed their families and, in the process, lost everything. They were forced into homelessness. By the time of Jesus the process was far advanced. The family farmer had lost his land to large estates owned by absentee landlords, managed by stewards, and worked by slaves, sharecroppers and day laborers.

The final straw was to be so heavily in debt that even their coats were offered as collateral. Interesting, Jewish law required a creditor to return a debtor's coat to him by sundown because it also served as his blanket. What Jesus taught was that when you have sunk to the lowest, are dragged into court and humiliated by losing your coat, Jesus said, *"Give them your cloak as well."* The cloak was the only undergarment that was worn. When you took off your cloak, you were naked as the day you were born! In effect, the debtor was saying, "You want my coat? Here, take everything. Now, all I have left is my naked body. Do you want that too?"

Jesus taught the poor to turn the tables and to clown. Nudity was taboo in Judaism. Can you see the crowds laughing, not just at the naked one, but also at the lender, the one who caused the nakedness! Embarrass the system, Jesus taught. Ridicule the system. Have you noticed that tyrants usually have no sense of humor? They abhor people laughing at them. Jewish people traditionally have a terrific sense of humor. It is no accident that many of our best comedians are Jewish! There is an old Jewish teaching, "If your neighbor calls you an ass, put a saddle on your back." Don't let people humiliate you, Jesus is saying. Turn the tables. Use humor. Put them in a position where they are ridiculed. Disarm them.

Go the second mile

The third example on how to turn the tables, take the initiative and keep the initiative is Matthew 5:41, *"If anyone forces you to go one mile, go also the second mile."* Usually we understand this to mean generosity. If someone asks you to do something for him or her, do even more than what they ask. When you understand the culture in which Jesus is teaching, you realize this is not at all what Jesus meant.

Note the word "force." Who could force you to go one mile? Roman soldiers had the right to impose forced labor on the locals, but under strict conditions. Rome well knew that they could push people only so far before there would be insurrection. Therefore, the law stated that a soldier could require a civilian to carry his heavy pack one mile, but only one mile. If a soldier forced the civilian to carry his pack more than one mile, the soldier would be severely disciplined.

What did Jesus teach? Get the soldier in trouble by going the second mile! Can you see the soldier, leisurely walking the first mile, enjoying his freedom, watching the civilian do his work for him. Then they reach the mile marker, and the civilian keeps walking.

"Hey! What are you doing?"

"Oh, it's a nice day. The sun is shining. The grass is green. I'm enjoying my walk. I'll just walk on further."

"Oh no, you don't. Put that pack down." Can you see the soldier frantically waving his arms trying to stop the civilian, hoping no one sees the infraction and report him to the Centurion?

*   *   *

When subjected to harassment and intimidation, turn the tables. Don't fight on their terms and with their methods. Don't do to them what they did to you. Don't retaliate in kind. Be creative, be innovative. Do something that gets them laughed at or gets them in trouble! Do something that immobilizes the perpetrator, that disarms him or her. The "slapper" had no recourse. If he did anything, he would lose his superior status by treating his slave or wife as an equal. The creditor had no recourse. The poor man gave him his coat. The lender was subjected to humiliation and could do nothing but endure the laughter. The soldier was rendered helpless. He was already in trouble with the centurion by forcing a local to go more than one mile. He could hardly further reprimand or punish the walker.

Jesus taught his followers not to resist by reacting on the perpetrator's terms, but to diffuse the situation and disarm the perpetrator. Rather than flee (submission, passivity, withdrawal, surrender) or fight (revolt, rebellion, retaliation, revenge), be creative, use humor, stand your ground, take control, don't react on the perpetrator's terms, diffuse the situation and disarm the perpetrator.

I'm indebted to Walter Wink for these interpretations. He demonstrated them in a fascinating workshop and wrote about them in two books: *Violence and Nonviolence in South Africa: the Third Way,* and *The Powers that Be: Theology for a New Millennium.*

*   *   *

In 1982, Ellie, our youngest son Craig, and I went to England. Craig, 15 years old, was not exactly thrilled to be traveling with his parents. We knew that if he sat in the back seat, he would read a book and be quite oblivious to the scenery, so we made him the navigator and sat him in the front next to me. With map in his hand, off we went. When Craig said, "Turn left at the next corner," my logic said to turn right, so I reacted as usual and stormed, "What do you mean left? That can't be the way. We need to turn right." Usually Ellie, as navigator, would argue back and off we would go in typical marital style! Craig, however, refused to resist. He refused to get into it. He refused to argue back. He refused to respond on my terms, using my method. He calmly replied, "All I do is give the directions. What you do with them is up to you." I was completely disarmed. He took the wind out of my sails. The situation was diffused. Meekly I turned left, and of course he was right! I relaxed and was quiet the rest of the trip. We had a wonderful time, and we all learned a great lesson, which I now realize is what Jesus taught. Don't argue back! Don't react on their terms. By the way, Craig is now a successful corporate attorney!

Turn the tables. Take the initiative, keep the initiative. Be creative, innovative and courageous. That's what Jesus meant.

2) Be assertive. Take the initiative

Jesus is not saying that we are to be pushovers. Jesus was certainly assertive, especially when it came to standing up for people who were being hurt, mistreated and taken advantage of by the pushy people.

In the Church of the Holy Sepulcher in Jerusalem, our group was patiently standing in line waiting to go into the shrine the Orthodox Church has built over the alleged site of the empty tomb from which Jesus was resurrected. This is a holy place for Christians, a place where the power of God was demonstrated for all time. We were patiently standing in line and approaching the entrance when a large group of German tourists walked up to us as if they were passing through. Our group parted to let them go through; only, to our surprise, they stopped. They had crashed the line, bypassing at least 50 people and dividing our group. Pushy people! My gentle wife, who quickly becomes assertive when pushy people attempt to take advantage of other people, put out her elbows and slowly backed up, pushing the Germans to the side, and allowing those in our group who had been pushed back, to retake their positions!

CHAPTER FOURTEEN

When People Are "Different"

"I'll go . . ." took me to different countries and exposure to people who were different from isolated, rural me. I soon learned that people are the same the world over, and prejudice, bigotry and intolerance are the results of fear—fear of something different, fear of people who are different. The current fear and intolerance of Muslims are yet another chapter in the history of ignorance. Narrow views, narrow perspectives, narrow circles of relationships need to be broadened. Be open to adventure. Be open to meeting new people, different cultures, customs and beliefs.

We used to think the world began at our borders. Jesus told us, *"Go into all the world and preach the gospel."* John Wesley preached, *"The world is my parish."* We thought the world was somewhere beyond our borders, and when we left the borders of the United States, we would encounter cultures, customs, values, life styles, philosophies different from our own. But now we do not need to leave our borders. Truly the world is now at our doorstep and it is imperative for us to overcome fear and prejudice and embrace the world which is our parish.

The Japan experience

After I graduated from college, I served in Nagoya, Japan, as a short-term missionary teacher at Nagoya Gakuin, a Methodist Junior and Senior Boys' High School. What a broadening, enriching, expanding experience for this farm boy from rural Minnesota.

The first week I almost starved to death, until I learned how to use chop sticks and how to fill up on rice without meat and potatoes. I learned how to eat and enjoy raw fish. I learned how to leave my shoes at the door and sit on the floor. I learned how to bow. I learned to converse in a language other than English.

It was a shared experience. I shared with the Japanese students a God who loves them just as they are. In a society where suicide is a common phenomenon, I shared with them how God loves them, how God values their lives, and how there is hope for their future.

And I learned much from the Japanese.

I learned tolerance.

I learned understanding and appreciation of another culture.

I learned about respect and order.

I observed a culture that is holistic in its approach, rather than the dissecting of children into school, home, church, and neighborhood as we do.

I discovered how indeed kids are the same the world over. They all play, tease, and misbehave. I discovered how people are all the same—we all love, weep, bleed, laugh.

American Indians

My first conversation with an American Indian occurred when I was in college and pastor of the two rural Minnesota Methodist churches. I was buying gasoline one day and noticed an old man wrapped in a blanket sitting behind the gas station. I asked who he was and learned he was Chief of the Chippewa tribe. He and I had a very interesting conversation but one thing he told me shocked my naive bones. He said, "The United States government has broken every treaty it made with Indians."

You may wonder why I use the word "Indian" rather than the politically correct word "Native American." One of our Merced Church members was a member of the Pawnee tribe in Oklahoma. I asked him what he thought of the phrase "Native American." He replied, "It's ridiculous. Anyone born in America is a native American!" The popular mystery author, Tony Hillerman, a Navajo from Albuquerque, wrote about a panel discussion in which the speakers were asked what they thought of the term "Native American."

They replied, "It's ridiculous! Anyone born in America is a native American."

"What would you like to be called?"

"Identify us by our tribe. If I am a Pawnee, call me a Pawnee; if Navajo, call me a Navajo; if Apache, call me an Apache. If you don't know my tribe, call me an Indian."

To which the Navajo commented, "We're just glad Columbus didn't think he had discovered Turkey!"

103

African Americans

The second year of field work experience while I was at Garrett was in downtown Chicago at The Methodist Church of the Redeemer. The stately brick edifice received that grand title when the original neighborhood was Italian. It was now an African-American neighborhood, and the church held all services, meetings and youth group on Sundays in the daytime. No one went out at night!

I led a teacher training class on Saturday mornings. Ellie taught a young children's Sunday School class and had to adapt the Methodist curriculum when she learned from one lesson that the children couldn't visualize a cow!

The hospitality mat was rolled out. We were entertained royally in several homes and on most Sundays were invited to have dinner with the pastor's family—Chuck, his wife Willie, and their two preschool boys. The parsonage was next door to the church. It was memorable to spend time with them before the afternoon meetings.

We enjoyed one unforgettable dinner and visit with Carrie, who told us of how she had grown up in the south with the renowned singer Marian Anderson. When we sat down at her table loaded with a sumptuous feast, she spread her hands and said, "Now, make your meal." In years since, we have often repeated the phrase. At the time of Marian Anderson's retirement, we attended a farewell concert in Minneapolis where it brought dear memories of Carrie.

Clifford and Nettie, a delightful young couple, invited us to a special Sunday afternoon concert by a community choir in which Clifford sang. We, the only white folks, were purposely ushered to the front row where he could watch our reaction! We wondered about the presence of uniformed nurses until the fainting started during the ecstatic frenzied clapping, swaying, dancing, screaming. Months later at a party at our house, Clifford laughed uproariously as he told how Ellie's big blue eyes got bigger and bigger!

A member of our Merced church was a retired school bus driver. During one kindergarten run, a little black girl sat behind him and talked. Oh, she loved to talk. She talked all the way to school and she talked all the way home, day after day. But one day she didn't say a word. He asked her if she was okay. She said, "I've been thinking. I think we should get married, and I will have two babies—a white one for you and a black one for me."

An innocent child's fantasy of peace and harmony— how sad that such innocence is soon victim to prejudice and fear.

Laotians

Recent immigrants from Laos worshiped in Modesto Church's chapel. Yona, the leader, was hired as the church custodian and thirty years later was still faithfully performing his duties. Randy helped with their worship services. When Elsie suggested a project to involve Laotian women, she and Ellie organized a quilting fellowship where women from both congregations sat around a quilting frame, visiting and stitching together.

Tongans

In the fall of 1983, a group of Tongans asked if they could hold services in Palo Alto's chapel. The Tongans are recent immigrants from the island of Tonga where Methodism is the dominant religion. The King and Princess of Tonga visited Palo Alto, worshiped with us and greeted the congregation.

The Tongans soon outgrew the chapel and began holding afternoon services in the sanctuary, as well as early Sunday morning services in the chapel.

Tongans enjoy lavish luaus, and our congregation was often invited. Barbecued in the parking lot, a pig with its head intact and taro root yams were staples.

The cultural differences proved challenging! There were messes from the luaus, children running in and out of the long worship services, carrying and eating snacks in the sanctuary! But we adapted; the children didn't!

Joint services were often held with the unique Tongan choir raising the roof. My, how they can sing!

We learned much from each other. From the Tongans, we learned about family solidarity and unity. We experienced different food. We learned to appreciate different clothing styles. Tongan Christian men combine two cultures in their dressing. They wear the shirt, tie and coat of the early British Methodist missionaries who converted Tonga to Methodism, but they retain the native skirt with bare feet, which make a great deal of sense in a hot climate such as Tonga.

In 1989, 113 Tongans became members of Palo Alto church. They have since organized their own United Methodist Church but continue to meet in our building. There have been splinter groups, but the congregation remains strong.

Fijians

Then Fijians arrived and began holding services in the chapel. Scheduling logistics was competently handled by our Church Administrator.

Fijian men enjoyed the kava drinking ceremony sitting on the floor. Surrounding a large wooden bowl filled with the yaqona beverage, they drank the muddy brown-colored liquid from half of a coconut shell. Yaqona has a calming effect (I drank some). Were they drinking an alcoholic beverage in a Methodist church? My position: Don't ask, don't tell!

Both Fiji and Tonga were war-like and cannibalistic until they were converted by British Methodist missionaries.

Hmongs

In Merced Church, we had a congregation of Hmongs who worshiped in their own language. When he was securing licensing and grants for our After School Ministry, Patrick interviewed the principal of Charles Wright School across the street. The makeup of Charles Wright School was revealing: 40% of the students were Hmong Americans, 33% were Mexican Americans, and the remaining 27% were "other," including Caucasians! The world was at our doorstep.

When I was a teenager, one of the highlights each year was to go to the St. Paul Auditorium to see the extravaganza on missions presented by the St. Paul Bible Institute, a school of the Christian Missionary Alliance denomination. The staging, lights, costumes, and music were outstanding as they told the story and presented the challenge of going into all the world with the good news. The program ended with the auditorium gradually darkening, with a spotlight on a person singing the song, *"Only one life to offer, Take it, dear Lord, I pray; Nothing from Thee withholding, Thy will I now obey,"* followed by a call to commitment to go to the mission field. The challenges strongly influenced my calls to become a missionary and a pastor.

Of course at the time I didn't understand the significance, but I like to think that I heard mission work among Hmongs at those services. I wouldn't have recognized the word "Hmong." They were people far, far away from Minnesota. It was Christian Missionary Alliance missionaries who proclaimed the good news to the Hmong people in the mountainous area of what is now Laos.

Wang Pao Thao was pastor of our Hmong congregation. His grandfather was a respected shaman among the Hmong people in Laos. During one festival while he was conducting a sacrifice, lightning hit the animal. Pastor Wang's grandfather immediately stopped the sacrifice, believing it was a sign that what he was doing was wrong. He further had a vision in which people of white skin (which he had never seen) would come to tell him about the true God and how God should be worshiped and served. Years later, missionaries came. Grandfather was ready for them. Grandfather received them and believed. Since that time his clan, including Pastor Wang, have been Christians. It was the missionaries who developed a written language for Hmong. The missionaries learned the language, put it into writing and translated the Bible.

The Hmong people have a history that strongly resembles the history of Jewish people. The Hmongs had no homeland and were often persecuted by the people around them. They moved from Mongolia (hence the word "Hmong") down into mainland China and lived there for centuries under terrible persecution. Some of them, to escape the persecution, moved to Laos where they were allowed to live isolated in the mountains, supporting themselves by primitive farming. They lived in relative peace until the CIA recruited some of them during the Vietnam War, including Pastor Wang, to form a secret army. Pastor Wang suffered wounds from a grenade in that war. When the Communists took over Laos, they began executing Hmongs because of their involvement with the U. S. Many of them escaped across the Mekong River into Thailand where they lived in refugee camps until our government relocated some of them to America. About half were refused admission.

Dang Moua went to the library in Richmond, Virginia and researched prevailing climates, soil conditions and crop yields. He chose Merced and the wave of immigration began. Like European and Asian immigrants, Hmongs stayed together. Today a sizable population of Hmongs live in Merced. A persecuted people without a homeland like the Jews who preserved their identity through the centuries, Hmongs arrived at our doorstep and the Hmong congregation grew.

The Spirit Catches You and You Fall Down: A Hmong Child, Her American Doctors, and the Collision of Two Cultures is a 1997 book by Anne Fadiman that vividly describes a cultural and language barrier conflict that occurred in Merced.

*   *   *

Merced Church responded well to Christ's command to "go . . . and proclaim." One of the young people from our church, Nanette, became a short-term missionary to Bolivia where there is a growing Methodist denomination—poor but vital. Nanette proclaimed the good news while teaching nutrition.

Lights out!

The Chancel Choir, accompanied by an orchestra, presented a Christmas concert when the lights went out! A car had hit a transformer, and most of downtown Palo Alto lost power. Immediately candles appeared. I didn't even know the church had a supply of candles, but someone

110

knew where they were, and we had candlelight. Leroy Kromm, our Director of Music, disappeared, and we learned later that he had rushed to the nursery to check on the children.

When he reappeared, he proceeded without musical scores to direct the orchestra in Christmas carols. We sang and sang.

After the concert and the lights were back on, I talked to a group of German tourists who were astounded by the response. I asked why, and they explained that in Germany the audience would have sat quietly until the power was restored!

Differences within cultures

Not only are there cultural differences between people from different countries, but there are cultural differences between people from different areas of the same country. A good example occurred to me when Sirkku called early one morning to tell me that the Merced city parade was going to be held in a few days, and wouldn't it be good advertising if our church had a float. I wholeheartedly agreed and asked her if she would organize it. She did. The church had a float, and it was accomplished with no committee, board or council involvement!

My colleagues often asked how valley churches like Manteca, Modesto and Merced were different from Palo Alto First. My observation, "If someone in a Board meeting in the valley said the church needed a new broom, "Joe" would say that he was going downtown the next day and would be glad to buy one. The meeting would adjourn. In Palo Alto, however, questions would be raised: "How big a broom? A sweeping broom or a push broom? What kind of bristles? Where will the broom be stored? Who will be responsible for it?" Then the issue would be referred to a committee for its input and the same questions would be gone over! I shared this metaphor with the United Church of Christ pastor in Palo Alto, and he said the same routine happens in his church. "It's the Silicon valley engineer syndrome," he analyzed.

Another cultural difference: At church potlucks in Minnesota, someone would say, "Oh pastor, you go first." In California, however, it's every man for himself! I soon learned to say grace while standing next to the table.

CHAPTER FIFTEEN

People First

A United Methodist woman pastor in Pennsylvania announced to her congregation that she was lesbian and that she had a partner. Charges were brought against her and the Conference withdrew her orders. However, her church hired her to continue ministry as a layperson.

In Pennsylvania, a United Methodist pastor officiated at his son's same-sex marriage. Charges were brought against him. He was found guilty of breaking church law, and his credentials were taken from him.

In Texas, a United Methodist pastor denied church membership to a gay man. Charges were brought against the pastor, but the Judicial Council (the Supreme Court of our denomination) decided in the pastor's favor, saying he did not violate church law.

Homosexuality is a controversy that is dividing the United Methodist Church. How do we deal with controversy biblically? In particular, homosexuality. Behind the conflict over the rights and status of homosexual persons is an ancient and deep-seated disagreement about the role of the Bible in our faith and practice and the interpretation of the Bible. What is the

113

authority of the Bible? How do we understand and apply the Bible to us today?

I join with those United Methodists who subscribe to the historic Wesleyan traditional belief in the authority of the Bible. 2 Timothy 3:16, *"All scripture is inspired by God."*

Therefore, because the Bible has authority over us, what about troublesome passages like:

Leviticus 11:2-8 forbids the eating of rabbits and pigs.

Leviticus 12 forbids a woman who has given birth to a son from going to church for 33 days because she is impure. If she gives birth to a girl, she is impure for 66 days!

Leviticus 20:13, *"If a man lies with a male as with a woman, both of them have committed an abomination; they shall be put to death."*

Deuteronomy 12:18, 21, *"If someone has a stubborn and rebellious son who will not obey his father and mother...Then all the men of the town shall stone him to death."*

Leviticus 20:10, *"If a man commits adultery with the wife of his neighbor, both the adulterer and the adulteress shall be put to death."*

1 Corinthians 11:5, *"Any woman who prays or prophesies with her head unveiled disgraces her head."*

Psalm 15:1,5, *"O Lord, who may abide in your tent? Who may dwell on your holy hill?... Those who do not lend money at interest."* (Where would America's economy be if we took that seriously?)

114

Do you know anyone who obeys all these passages? It is obvious that all Christians use some method by which they decide which verses and passages have more authority than others. Let's look at some methods of biblical interpretation.

1) **"Pick and Choose"** is the most popular form of biblical interpretation. Pick out the passages with which we agree, and discard the rest. This method assumes the Bible has no inherent authority. Whatever agrees with our biases, prejudices and what we want to do is chosen, the rest discarded. Whatever one agrees with has more authority than the Bible. Those of us who believe in the authority of the Bible must reject the Pick and Choose method.

2) The **"All or Nothing"** method assumes that every word is literally written by God, and every word is authoritative. If some passages are questioned, then the entire Bible is in question. Such believers, however, are rarely consistent. Do the women wear head coverings? Do they throw stones at their misbehaving children? Do they lend money at interest? We must reject the All or Nothing method as unworkable and not even followed by its own adherents.

3) The **"Filter"** or historical method is the method I recommend. God did not write the words of the Bible directly, but wrote through people. The Bible covers a period of about 2,000 years—from Abraham through the early church. There are different cultures reflected in the Bible from the nomadic Hebrews to the sophisticated Greek culture of the Roman Empire. There are many filters to

work through. Many of the troublesome passages can be attributed to cultural filters, and therefore do not have authority over us.

4) The "**People First**" method. When deciding what is authoritative and what is not, what criteria do we use? Our own ideas, our own cultural bias, modern science? I believe I have come to a conclusion which I hope will be helpful for the church. As Christians who follow Jesus as Lord, who recognize Jesus Christ as the cornerstone of our faith, we attempt to understand and look through Jesus' filter. Jesus Christ is our ultimate authority, and Jesus put PEOPLE FIRST.

In the current controversy over homosexuality, there are many United Methodists who are quite passionate about the few Bible verses that condemn homosexual behavior. They are also quite passionate about our denomination's position, which accepts homosexuals as "individuals of sacred worth" but condemns "the practice of homosexuality." I don't understand the distinction. It's as if we accept tennis players, but they are forbidden to play tennis. Or we accept swimmers, but they are not allowed to swim. We accept homosexuals, but they can't act like one!

Also, the official position of our denomination— "fidelity in marriage, and celibacy in singleness"—is cruel. No sex outside marriage sounds moral, but our denomination does not allow holy unions so gays are forever single by definition and therefore are commanded to be celibate. In 1943, Esther, from the Wesley congregation, left the Internment Camp in Washington and

116

went to Mississippi to marry her fiancé who was a soldier in the U.S. Army. They asked the Army chaplain to marry them, but he refused because they were Japanese! Imagine. (But the local Methodist minister, with many of his congregation in attendance, married them!) Isn't it equally tragic for the United Methodist Church to prohibit gays from forming holy unions and thereby forcing them into singleness and celibacy? It's easy for married heterosexuals to condemn gays to celibacy. Easy and cruel.

United Methodist legalists are quite passionate about their beliefs but are either ignorant of or do not care how their beliefs affect people; how homosexuals are hurt by the church laws. We are not putting people first.

Jesus was impatient with the legalists of his day.

Jesus cared about the man with the withered hand and healed him even though it meant violating the Sabbath laws.

Jesus cared more about the need of his disciples to eat than he cared about the Sabbath law.

Jesus cared more about the rights of women who could be divorced easily than he cared about the sanctity of the holy Mosaic scriptural law.

There is no record that Jesus ever said anything about homosexuality.

But I believe Jesus cares more about gays and lesbians than he cares about the Social Principles of the United Methodist Church!

Jesus put people first.

The last six of the Ten Commandments can be summarized: Love your neighbor by putting people first. If we truly put people first, there would be no stealing, no murder, no adultery, no coveting, etc.

By the inspiration of the Holy Spirit, the criterion by which we decide what in the Bible is authoritative and what in the *United Methodist Book of Discipline* is authoritative is that we, following Jesus, put people first.

We're not just talking about laws, principles and Biblical interpretation; we're talking about people—real, live human beings who hurt, who suffer, who struggle with their lives, trying to fit in, trying to belong, doing the best they can, wondering why they are the way they are, sometimes agonizing why God made them the way they are.

We're not just talking about people in the news or demonstrating on the street, we're talking about people we know, people in our families (most families have a gay person somewhere). We're talking about people in the church—people who have been raised in the church. People, I believe, Jesus puts first.

"Will you baptize my triplets"?

A young man phoned, "I would like to arrange a private baptism for my triplets." I explained to him that according to United Methodist polity, we do not conduct private baptisms. Through baptism, children become part of God's family—the church—and the church family witnesses,

118

rejoices in the baptism and promises to support the child in his or her spiritual development.

While we were talking, I checked the Paradise Valley Church directory and found his name listed as a constituent. United Methodist policy also states that the parents must be members of the church. I have disregarded that rubric as I believe baptism is between God and the children. The parents' lack of faith should not be a hindrance or obstacle between God and the child.

At some point in the conversation, he told me he had a partner who was also father of the triplets. I gulped and said, "Let me come and visit." We set up a time.

I went to their home, met the two fathers and smiled at the adorable six-month old triplets—a boy and two girls. James and Jeff told me their story. They had arranged for a surrogate mother in San Diego to carry and give birth. Such a procedure is against the law in Arizona, so they went to California. The triplets were born early and remained in the hospital for over a month. The Dads alternated visits.

After they were brought home to Phoenix, one of the nurses flew to check on the babies whom she had come to adore!

I asked how they were being received by the neighbors. "Just fine; they are very supportive." "How about your parents?" I learned that Jeff's father had died, but his mother had moved to Phoenix to help care for the children. Jeff and his mother were Presbyterians in Michigan.

I asked James how his parents were responding. He sadly said that he and his family were Methodists in Texas.

I thought to myself, "Oh, no!" Sure enough, when he "came out," his parents reacted strongly and practically disowned him. They refused to accept the relationship. After the babies were born, his parents told him, "That is sinful. The Christian thing to do is to put them up for adoption."

When we returned to the subject of baptism, I said, "I agree that the baptism should be private rather than during a worship service but with a few representatives of the congregation in attendance." I explained that I was the Interim Senior Pastor and would not have the opportunity to prepare the congregation or be available for follow-up. I said that I would phone the new pastor who would be coming in a few months. "If he is not supportive, you won't want to continue coming to this church." They agreed.

I returned to my office, phoned the new pastor who immediately responded that he would be very supportive and encouraged me to proceed with the baptism. I called together the other pastors on the staff. They all immediately agreed that I should proceed. I phoned the Lay Leader/Chair of the Administrative Council. He concurred. I phoned the chair of the Staff-Parish Relations Committee (the personnel committee). He agreed enthusiastically. I then invited them and a few others to attend and represent the congregation.

What a moving, beautiful, unforgettable service we had! We held it in the chapel on a Saturday morning. On one side sat Grandma, the children's nanny, some neighbors, and the church representatives. On the other side, sat row after row of young men, some from Texas! There wasn't a dry eye. Ellie and Paula, the wife of the Staff-Parish Relations Chair, hosted a reception following the service, a grand celebration.

About a year later, I saw James and Jeff on the patio following a Sunday service and I asked them how they were doing. James exclaimed, "My Dad phoned and emotionally said he didn't want the children to wonder why their grandfather didn't like them!" They reconciled and the grandparents now play an active role in the triplets' lives. God is good!

Truly, God's amazing love embraces everyone. Jesus loves the little children—all the children.

A holy covenant

In 2006, two young women asked me to bless their partnership. They had been living together for some time and wanted to ask God's blessing in a church setting. I was retired at the time, living part-time in Walnut Creek, California. Because of the United Methodist position, I did not want to compromise the United Methodist pastor so we held the ceremony in the United Church of Christ sanctuary. There was a small congregation of family and friends, followed by dinner in a local restaurant.

I wrote the following Welcome which gives the theological context for the celebration: *"We are gathered together in the sight of God to witness and bless the joining together of Stephanie and Eva. You are created in the image of God who created you in love that you might love one another, embraced by the faithful love of God. The presence and power of Jesus Christ is with you today. With His sacrificial love for the world, Jesus set before us his life-giving example for all human relationships. We look to that example today for the sustaining love of your covenant. Through the Holy Spirit who called you together and has walked with you to this moment, you have come to give yourselves to one another in this holy covenant."*

Wesley Church action

October 21, 2013, in opposition to the official United Methodist position on homosexuality, the congregation with a unanimous vote adopted the following resolution:

Wesley United Methodist Church proclaims, without reservation, God's unconditional love and grace and affirms the dignity and worth of every person as created in the image of God. We are a Reconciling Congregation welcoming into the full life of the church all persons regardless of age, ethnicity, economic circumstance, gender identity and sexual orientation. We welcome all who wish to worship God.

I wrote to Keith Inouye, the Senior Pastor, and congratulated him on his courageous and capable leadership. He replied:

Thank you Doug! But on the contrary; when I first came to Wesley UMC many folks shared with me how much you advocated all of this from the pulpit during your time serving here. My brother Larry especially appreciated your directness in telling it as you saw it and my mother in reflecting upon what she remembered you said shared with me, "and I agreed with Rev. Norris, I believe that too!" You helped sow many seeds of insight, boldness, and compassion here! Thank you for laying much faithful groundwork!

*   *   *

When people are "different," realize that they are created and loved by God. We dare not do less. When people seem different to you, realize that you seem different to them.

CHAPTER SIXTEEN

Where Was God When the Freeway Fell?

"Where was God when . . . ?" is a question that has bothered human beings throughout history. However, the Loma Prieta earthquake that shocked the San Francisco Bay Area in 1989 convinced me that this is the wrong question to ask. Because these are the wrong questions, no wonder the answers traditional theology have given are so inadequate. It sometimes takes earthquakes to shake us out of our stupor and face reality. Did your mother ever shake you to get your attention? You weren't paying any attention to what she was saying, so she took you by the shoulders, shook you, looked into your eyes and said, "Listen to me!" An earthquake is the way the earth releases pressure. An earthquake might also be the way Mother Nature shakes us to get our attention, "Listen to me!"

2 Thessalonians 3:3, *"The Lord is faithful; he will strengthen you and guard you from evil."* The Lord is faithful and will guard you. But what about those who lost their lives in the 1989 earthquake? Where was God when the freeway fell? Why did some die? Why were some saved? Will God take care of you? The hymn, *"God will take care of you, through every day, o'er all the way,"* almost didn't get into the current United Methodist hymnal.

Several on the committee said it should be deleted. A seminary professor said the hymn is not only sentimental, but not always true.

Several of those who survived the freeway crash publicly thanked God for taking care of them, believing that God answered their desperate prayers. What about those whose prayers were not answered? What about those who lost their homes? Is God fair? Renae asked the children in Sunday School on Reformation Sunday to list important beliefs like Martin Luther did. One important belief the children have is, "God is never unfair." Are they right? Is God never unfair? If so, why do the good sometimes suffer and die young? Why do the bad guys seem to prosper? Why are there natural disasters?

The earthquake and the aftershocks had a sobering effect. People seemed to be in shock. Their energy level was low. Some were discouraged and depressed. Some were close to panic. It was good to talk with others about the stress we all felt. The earthquake also brought out the best in people. The crime rate was almost nonexistent for several days. People helped one another. For a few refreshing moments, priorities got straightened out. So many said, "I realize how unimportant things are." Or, "I learned how important my family is to me." According to an article, some businesses were concerned about the attitude of employees who were reevaluating how hard they were working; did it matter in the long run! The earthquake did shake us and got our attention.

What is the message?

What is being said to us through the earthquake? THE PLANET ON WHICH WE LIVE HAS A LIFE OF ITS OWN, NOT CENTERED ON US. The earth is not in existence for us. We are not the owners of this planet. We are guests. We are strangers. We are foreigners. We are only visiting for a while. Like a Star Trek episode where the heroes battle unfriendly elements on a distant planet, that distant planet is actually the earth. The earth is not always friendly. It is our egos that get us into trouble!

*   *   *

The pastor of All Saints' Church, wrote in his newsletter that the earth in all its wonder is "our fragile island home." It is both fragile and immensely powerful. It is our friend but, if we don't respect it and its natural laws, the earth can be our enemy. It is the only place we have and we are dependent upon it. It is a gift from God and a reminder of God's almighty power, faithfulness, and love. The planet on which we live has a life of its own, not centered on us.

*   *   *

The Christian Century magazine published a fascinating article before the earthquake, "*Fierce Landscapes and the Indifference of God*," by Belden C. Lane. Professor Lane observes how the land in which people live affect their beliefs. People who live in the sparse Sinai desert, the austere Scottish Highlands, and the stark Tibetan mountains have encountered a God of fierce indifference. By this he means the Old Testament Jews, Tibetan Buddhists, and Scottish Calvinist Presbyterians, because of a hostile environment, learned how to live with God and survive an unfriendly earth. They developed a rigorous, fierce, tough, resilient faith and life style.

Lane contrasts their theology with that of America where we have mixed popular psychology with a theology wholly devoted to self-realization, a theology that lets us down when earthquakes shake.

"I really don't want a God who is solicitous of my every need, fawning for my attention, eager for nothing in the world so much as the fulfillment of my self-potential. One of the scourges of our age is that all of our deities are housebroken and eminently companionable; far from demanding anything, they ask only how they can more meaningfully enhance the lives of those they serve."

*   *   *

We tend to have it backwards, trying to find gods who will serve us, rather than we serving the transcendent God who, along with the earth, is not dependent on us! This article, written before the earthquake, helps me understand how our religion, especially for those who live in California, is shaped by a warm climate, surrounded by the beauty of Yosemite and the ocean and influenced by a Hollywood culture. Too many of us have fallen into the error, even heresy, of believing that God's sole purpose is

128

to keep us happy and provide us with pleasure. We want a Zsa Zsa Gabor religion: everything my way! Or a Frank Sinatra religion: "I did it my way." We seem to believe if we think positively enough and pray, everything will work to our benefit. And when it doesn't, we can't understand it. We are disillusioned and depressed, asking irrelevant questions like why do the good suffer, and where was God when the freeway fell?

We live in earthquake country and wonder why there are quakes. Many wise people before us, including Jesus, warned us about the foolish man who built his house on the sand. Sooner or later, a child who plays with fire will get burned. And when he gets burned, do you blame the match? Or ask, where was God when he got burned? Or, why do little boys suffer? Those questions are irrelevant. We live in earthquake country where freeways fall.

*   *   *

American pioneers had a tough religion for their austere conditions. They knew they lived on an unfriendly earth. They battled the elements, battled unfriendly nature, and were grateful for their victories. They expected, and here is the difference from us, the land to be unfriendly. They expected tornadoes and floods. They expected hail and pestilence. They expected disease and death. They recognized their vulnerability in the face of nature and their utter dependence on God. They recognized how much they depended on God for deliverance and blessings, for good weather and good crops.

And they praised God and thanked God when they were delivered. They rejoiced, praised and thanked God when they didn't die, rather than feeling cheated when a loved one did die. They gathered in the churches, they gathered at thanksgiving feasts to praise God when there was a harvest. How many were in church following the earthquake to thank God for their survival? How many are grateful to God for every breath they breathe, for every drink of clean water they take?

The earthquake shook us up and got our attention. The planet on which we live has a life of its own, not centered on our plans and desires. The earth is friendly at times, but the givens are earthquakes, storms, tornadoes, hurricanes, cancer, disease, death. Why should we be surprised when death occurs? Why should we be surprised and question why the good die young? Why should we wonder why some survive and some don't? The surprise is that some survive! Praise God! The surprise is that many houses did not fall. Praise God! The surprise is that not everyone dies young. Praise God! The surprises are evidence that God is faithful, God will strengthen you and guard you from evil.

*   *   *

No, the questions to ask are not: where was God when the freeway fell? Why do some survive and some don't? Why do the righteous and the young die? The questions to ask are: how do we get along with God? How do we live on this earth where earthquakes, tornadoes, fires, cancer, plagues are indiscriminate, where the victims may be good, righteous and young? Then we are led to the answer: in humble dependence upon the God of nature who, through prayer and faith, gives us the courage, strength, and resilience to fight the elements, take up the challenge and risk, expecting evil, death, earthquakes, and taxes; and expressing gratitude to God for the victories and surprises.

With this outlook and belief system, we will discover on a very deep level that God is faithful, God will strengthen, guard and protect. That's the promise. At a deeper level than what things we want, a deeper level than our pleasure and happiness, a deeper level than our self-importance and fulfillment, a deeper level than the battle with an unfriendly earth, a deeper level than life and death is the promise, the assurance, that your salvation is in Christ, and God will take care of you.

"God will take care of you, through every day, o'er all the way." During the debate in the Hymnal Committee over whether the hymn *God Will Take Care of You* should be included in the new hymnal, a woman who had come into United Methodism from a Lutheran background, said, *"This hymn is not in any Lutheran hymnal. It does not meet my objective standards for good music or a good text. But when my Lutheran grandmother was dying, this was the hymn she wanted sung to her. What I remember about it at the time was the extravagance—more than what made good sense—of God's love and care that was promised."* On a level deeper even than death, her grandmother knew that God will take care of her.

The planet on which we live has a life of its own, not centered on us, but God will take care of us. 2 Thessalonians 3:3: *"The Lord is faithful; he will strengthen you and guard you from evil."*

We have little or no control over nature, but what humans do to themselves and one another is another matter.

CHAPTER SEVENTEEN

How Mighty Is Almighty?

Did God plan everything that has happened? Is God in complete control? Is everything that happens God's will? Was the Holocaust, where 6 million human beings were slaughtered by the Nazis, God's will? Was the killing of some 160 innocent children, men and women in the Oklahoma City bombing God's will? Was the bombing predestined? Was 911 God's will? Was the Newtown massacre God's will? Was it God's will that the dangerous respiratory virus, RSV, put my twin granddaughters in the hospital? I certainly believe it was God's will that they are made well; but is disease God's will? Billy Graham was asked what he would tell parents whose children had been killed. He replied, "It was God's will." Was it?

To state the dilemma theologically—and these questions have been debated for centuries—if God is in control, then God is responsible for evil; therefore God is not good. On the other hand, if God is not responsible for evil, and did not will the Holocaust, and does not will cancer or RSV, then God is good but not almighty. There is the dilemma—how mighty is almighty?

In charge but not in control

I find it helpful to make the distinction between "in charge" and "in control." God is in charge, but not in control. The Bishop appointed me as Senior Pastor. As the senior pastor, I am in charge of the staff; but I'm certainly not in control! A principal is in charge of a school, but he or she cannot control what goes on in the school. Queen Elizabeth reigns but she can't control her subjects. Our God reigns, but does not control. God is in charge of the planet, but does not control humanity.

Why? Three reasons:

1) God is constantly creating order out of chaos. According to the first chapter of Genesis, God created the world out of chaos, and God is still creating order out of chaos. Chaos is not yet under control. Cancer, where cells are out of control, and order needs to be restored, is an example of chaos. Cancer is not God's will.

2) Human beings have free will. We can choose right or wrong, love or hate, good or evil. We can choose to ignore God and to oppose God. When we choose to oppose God, are we not responsible for the consequences of our actions? How can we say it is God's fault?

3) There is evil. Call it what you will—the devil or evil or a force—evil is constantly attacking, constantly trying to undo what is good, thwarting the will of God. *"The devil prowls around like a roaring lion looking for someone to devour."* (1 Peter 5.8) Bill Cosby was asked if he thought his son's murder was God's will. He replied, "No, the devil

134

walked with the murderer." Matthew 4:11 records the conflict between Jesus and the devil. Following his baptism, Jesus went into the wilderness for forty days where he was tempted by the devil. Even Jesus was confronted by the devil, even Jesus throughout his ministry had to contend with the forces of evil, and so must we.

*   *   *

God is in charge, but not in control because of chaos, free will and evil.

A ministry cut short

Four went into the ministry from the West Bethel youth group. Three others from the church, who had been too old for the youth group, followed later for a total of seven. Four of those who entered the ministry were Almquist brothers. Three stayed in Minnesota, but George went to Kansas, where he became a very successful pastor. He had an excellent singing voice and was a popular preacher. He wrote a manual on starting cooperative parishes. In 1978 George participated in a special Conference session in Wichita. Following the evening session, declining a ride, he started walking to the motel. But, he never got there. George was mugged and killed. He was only 43-years old.

Arsonist sets fire

In February 1996, a teenager high on drugs set fire to the Merced Mt. Pisgah AME (African Methodist Episcopal) Zion Church building. When I read of the fire in the morning paper, I immediately called the pastor, expressed my sympathy and support, and invited his congregation to use our buildings for services. For several months, they held a Sunday morning worship service in our Fellowship Hall, and we held several joint services featuring the Mt. Pisgah Youth Rap Choir. The AME Zion bishop preached twice and, wow, could he preach!

Billy Bunts, the pastor, and I became friends. When I retired, he gladly and gratefully took most of my library. My method of deciding which books to keep and which to give was simple: if I hadn't opened a book in the six years I was in Merced, I didn't need to keep it!

The exorcism

Returning home from an evening concert at 10:00 on July 6, 1997, there were three phone messages from "Carmen" (I've changed her name for confidentiality reasons) on the answering machine. "Pastor Doug, it is very important that I see you." I phoned her. Because she did not want to discuss her problem on the phone, I said I would be right over. Before I left, she called again and asked me to bring holy water.

I went by the church office, picked up my vial of olive oil that we use in healing services and arrived at her apartment at 10:30.

Carmen and her roommate, "Jane," met me at the door. Carmen's baby was with a grandmother as they were in the process of changing apartments. Most of the furniture had gone and there was a general mess.

The girls explained that they were frightened. Something weird was happening.

On the 4th of July evening, three of their friends (boys) were in the Bass Lake area when one, a 17-year-old, suggested they visit a friend of his to whom he was drawn and who was a practicing witch. The witch was entertaining her boyfriend and became angry with the 17-year old for coming and refused to let them in.

On the way home, the boy became violently ill. The driver pulled over to the side of the road. The 17-year old vomited a large amount in bright colors through the open window all over the side of the car. He then got out of the car, writhed in the ditch, shouted obscenities and spoke in tongues. The friends tried to get him into the car, but he refused, hollered at them and resisted them.

The two friends left him there, drove back to the witch's house and asked for her help. She refused. On their way home to Merced, the car lights began blinking and a tire blew out. They stopped to change the tire, and when they tried to start the car it would not start. They then walked to Merced (took four hours). No one would pick them up.

Later the two appeared at Carmen and Jane's apartment. When they entered, the girls said a presence of evil came with them.

The next day, the 17-year-old came to their apartment. The police had picked him up as he staggered along the highway. They kept him for the night. His sister went and brought him back to Merced. He had gone to the doctor and felt better; the girls, however, said his eyes were strange—he was not himself.

The girls were frightened. They heard noises. There was occasional tapping on the window. They felt a presence of evil. A friend brought over three Guardian Angel candles. The girls lit them and put them in the living room and the two bedrooms. When Carmen read from the Bible out loud, the living room candle burst into flames and damaged the glass container. The candle in Jane's room burned brightly without seeming to use wax. The candle in Carmen's room flickered rapidly. They also showed me the bed in Jane's room in which the boy sometimes slept. It had crashed to the floor!

I asked them how the presence felt. They used words like weird and scary. We stood in a circle holding hands and I prayed for God, in the name of Jesus, to cast out all alien, foreign, unfriendly, evil forces. I then took the oil and anointed each girl "In the name of the Father, Son, and Holy Spirit." Then I went to the front door, made the sign of the cross on the door case and said, "In the name of the Father, Son, and Holy Spirit"

I anointed the living room, Jane's bedroom and Carmen's room. When I anointed the door in Carmen's bedroom, the flickering candle stopped flickering! The girls, open-eyed, exclaimed, "Wow!"

Then I asked them to walk all around the apartment and wherever they felt uncomfortable, I repeated the anointing. I anointed the kitchen and the closet in Carmen's room. By this time, the candle had resumed flickering, but at a much slower pace. Jane asked me to anoint her bedroom window where the tapping had occurred. When I finished, the candle again had stopped flickering!

We returned to the living room. Asking them how they felt, they both smiled and said, "It feels good in here." I gave them the benediction and left.

A mother's worst nightmare

On March 26, 2002, Christine came home from her daily 7:00 morning walk with a friend to discover, to her horror, that her ex-husband had managed entry into the house, shot her three children, sat on Christine's bed, held their daughter on his lap, shot her and then himself!

We were now living in Gilbert, Arizona. Telephone calls from the Merced pastor and the Administrative Assistant apprised us of the unbelievable tragedy.

I had married the couple in the Merced church. In the premarital sessions, we had discussed some of the tension points between them. On the morning of the afternoon wedding, they sat in our living room. Christine shared her misgivings. We discussed his temper. After the rehearsal the previous evening, he had a quarrel with Christine's relatives, threw a tantrum and stormed out. He promised Christine and me that he would seek help and get counseling (which he did not do). I, of course, wish I had handled it differently. I wish I had been more forceful, but I did give them permission not to go through with the wedding. "We can have a party instead." But they decided to proceed.

139

Michelle, a darling baby girl was born, and I baptized her. Her father adored her, brought her to church regularly, but was not on the best of terms with Christine's children—Melanie, Stanley and Stuart, all teenagers. They were very talented, intelligent, attractive and popular. Ellie had taught the boys in Sunday School.

The funeral was held in the Roman Catholic Church, which had the largest sanctuary in the city. The children had attended the parochial elementary school. Four white caskets were lined up in front of the altar. Before the service, Christine came up to me and told me not to feel guilty. Imagine! She reached out to me in the midst of her sorrow.

The next morning I accompanied Christine to the crematorium. Later she wrote, *"If not for you, I don't know if I ever could have let them go through the cremation. Remember that morning? That haunts me. But you found the words to walk me through it. When I finally, finally was able to nod ok at the mortician, I was asked a final question: Did I have a preference in who went first? What order they went in? Oh dear God, dear God. Forever passed before I could whisper, "the boys. Send the boys first. They'll protect the girls on the other side." May God forgive me, may my children forgive me.*

No one can imagine what Christine went through. None of this "I know how you feel" or "I know what you are going through." No one knows! How Christine grieved and coped is inconceivable. She immediately reached out to Melanie's closest friends, creating opportunities for long-time mutual support. She appeared several times on Oprah and told her story. On the second appearance, she helped Oprah counsel others who were dealing with tragedy.

Christine remarried and gave birth to twin girls. The family live in Christine's house because, "the home is full of laughter and good memories." The house is full of photos of all her children.

After the twins were born, Christine wrote the following:

"How do you respond to the woman who looks at you across the table and with a heart full of sincerity says, 'When I cannot feel God working in my life I just look at you and see all of his goodness . . .'

What I did was smile back and mumble, 'thank you.'

What I wanted to do was reach across the table, grab her by the throat and shove her up against the wall, screaming the entire time 'NOOOOOOOOOOO! Goodness? NOOOO00000! Where was God when all four of my children died within inches of bibles by their beds? All four had personal bibles right next to their blown out brains! How can you give God credit NOW because I once again have children, but ignore the fact that . . .

You get my drift."

*   *   *

What to say and what not to say to one who is in deep grief is a dilemma we all face. It is better to listen than to speak hurtfully. It is certainly hurtful to speak when the one in grief has not opened the door! When in doubt, say nothing. It is better to say nothing than to attempt to make sense of another person's tragedy and grief.

On October 1, 2012, Ellie and I, with our good friends Dave and Sandra, visited Garrett-Evangelical Seminary in Evanston, Illinois. Dave and I also attended a class on pastoral counseling and I shared this experience with them. The Professor turned it into a long class discussion with class members reflecting on how they might have handled the premarital sessions. They also shared experiences of their own. The importance of counseling with fortunate or unfortunate consequences was verified.

I include this tragedy to encourage pastors to be aggressive in their pre-marital counseling; to be alert and sensitive to signals of trouble and then honestly, assertively share their concerns with the couple.

When I shared this writing of Christine's experience with her, she responded with this counsel: *"Speak up and be heard! Call it as you see it! Not quite the same as telling someone what to do, but truly expressing your discomfort - or enthusiasm - for whatever you witness in counseling."*

*   *   *

God is in charge, but not in control because of chaos, free will and evil.

CHAPTER EIGHTEEN

What Went Wrong? Why Is There Evil?

The message of the Bible is timeless. John 3:16, *"For God so loved the world that he gave his only Son, so that everyone who believes in him may not perish but may have eternal life."*

Does anyone doubt that perish is a real possibility? That our children may perish—individually and collectively; that civilization, even our planet may perish? That war, crime, violence, greed, pollution, nuclear disaster may eventually do us in? What is wrong? What went wrong? Why is perish a real possibility?

We look to the stories for answers. The stories in the first part of Genesis were told to answer the question, "What went wrong?" Genesis chapter one tells us God's creation is good; Genesis chapters 2-11 tell the stories of what went wrong, and what is still going wrong.

I highly recommend the book, *Ishmael,* by Daniel Quinn. It's one of those books you can't put down— fascinating and intriguing. Quinn divides humankind into two groups: civilized and primitive.

The primitives

The primitives have been on this earth for millions of years. They were and are hunters, gatherers and herdsmen.

143

Incidentally, I heard on the radio why men have trouble finding things. Our ancient ancestors were hunters and gatherers. The men were the hunters, and the women were the gatherers. The women learned how to look. They learned how to find that one last berry hiding on the bush, the last egg under the chicken. Men were the hunters. When I told my son Jack, he replied, "In other words, it has to move before we see it." As you stand in the open doorway of the refrigerator, how often has your wife said, "Well, does it have to jump out before you can see it?" Exactly!

The civilized

Back to the stories: The primitives are hunters, gatherers and herdsmen and have lived successfully for millions of years. About 10,000 years ago, an event occurred which forever changed history. Someone began farming. They began tilling the soil, which meant they had to stay in one place. They became very possessive of their land. They felt they owned the land. This in itself did not cause problems, for even the primitives guard their turf. The American Indians had tribal boundaries, and if they invaded their neighbors, a battle would ensue.

Possession of the land, preserving it for farming was not necessarily wrong, but when our ancestors began to expand their turf, a new phenomenon appeared on the face of the earth. The so-called civilized peoples began attacking and destroying the primitives, driving them off, confiscating the land. They began killing animals indiscriminately, not just when they needed to eat, as do the primitives. The civilized began stockpiling, hoarding their food. They became greedy, wanting more and more.

Not only did they want more and more, they felt it was their right to take. They felt it was their right to kill off the American Indian and the Australian Aboriginal and to steal the land. After all, they rationalized, "Our way of life is superior. We are civilized. They are only savages. We have a God-given right to the land. Everything belongs to us. All of creation belongs to us. And, we can do anything with it that we please." In that statement is the crux of what went wrong with civilization.

Back to the stories: Do you see who told the story of Cain and Abel? The story describes the ancient controversy between herdsmen and farmers.

According to herdsmen, God was not pleased with the agricultural offering. God was not pleased with the behavior of the civilized who were expanding their territory, destroying anything that got in their way. Cain killed Abel. And the descendants of Cain, namely so-called civilized people, are still killing Abel. We have destroyed tribes of people and driven the remnants to reservations. We have killed off entire species of animal and plant life without a second thought. We have destroyed rain forests without a thought of the effects on weather or the future of the planet.

Adam and Eve

The story of Cain and Abel describes what went wrong. The stories of Adam and Eve and the Tower of Babel tell us why. In the beginning, Adam blamed Eve and Eve blamed the serpent. The serpent was the cultic symbol of the Baal religion, which was a feminist fertility cult. So the Fall of Mankind is the fault of women and the Great Mother nature religions.

Adam and Eve lived like affluent primitives in the Garden of Eden; everything was provided. They could do what they pleased, and eat what they pleased, except the fruit of the tree of the knowledge of good and evil. The Lord God told them they would die if they ate that fruit. But the serpent tempted them by saying, Genesis 3:5, *"When you eat of it your eyes will be opened, and you will be like God, knowing good and evil."*

When the Lord God found out they had eaten of the fruit, they were kicked out of the garden. Genesis 3:23, *"Therefore the Lord God sent him forth from the garden of Eden, to till the ground."* The punishment was farming! Agriculture was the curse! Guess who told this story! Herdsmen! However, there are days when farmers might agree with them!

Tower of Babel

The story of the Tower of Babel is the story of civilized people building the first city, a city with a huge tower, its top in the heavens. And the Lord said, Genesis 11:6, *"This is only the beginning of what they will do; nothing that they propose to do will now be impossible for them."* This prophecy has certainly come true and is still coming true.

146

Nothing will be impossible for humankind. Even destroying ourselves, even perishing is now possible.

To be like God

To want to be like God and to act like God is what went wrong. To replace God as the provider and sustainer of life, to put ourselves in the #1 spot at the center of the universe, is what went wrong with civilization. We think we are god. We think the earth belongs to us, not that we belong to the earth. Somehow "dominion over the earth" in Genesis chapter one became conqueror and destroyer of the earth. We act as if it is our right to do with the earth as we please. We want more and more. What is wrong is to let greed run rampant. When is enough enough? How much does one need to live successfully?

What is wrong is to think and act as if the universe belongs to us. What is wrong is to think and act as if it is our right to decide who will live and who will die. Why are we threatened by people whose culture is different? Why do we try to change them, to "civilize" them? Why are we threatened by people whose lifestyle is different, who wear different clothes, or things in their ears and nose? Why are heterosexuals threatened by homosexuals? Why can't we all live on this planet together? Why not? Because we are insecure. Because we have replaced God with ourselves, we are not sure of ourselves and are threatened by anyone who is different. If we persist, we will perish.

God never gives up

But God is not willing to let us perish. God sent prophet after prophet to bring us back, back to the worship of the one true God, back to the values and morals taught and lived by Jesus. How we need a Savior! Civilization needs a Savior. You need a Savior to save you from greed that swallows you, to save you from a self-centered universe where those you love cannot live with you because of your ego, to save you from demanding that other people think and act like you do, to save you from destroying yourself with drugs or alcohol or gambling, to save you from destroying relationships with your egotism, selfishness and pride, to save you from perishing!

How we need a Savior! Praise God, we have one! God so loved the world he gave his only Son! It was for you Jesus came. It was for you Jesus died because God loves you. God loves you so much God was willing to make the supreme sacrifice for you and for the world, that none of us should perish, but have life, life here and now, and life eternal. Repent and receive the life Christ has for you. Put God back in the center and enter into partnership with God, co-operate with God in leading humankind to repentance before we all perish.

CHAPTER NINETEEN

I'll Go . . . on the Road Again

Deep in the heart of Texas

After my first few months at Garrett, a note on the seminary bulletin board announced that a graduate who was now the pastor in Rocksprings, Texas, and his wife would be traveling to the Holy Land and needed a summer substitute. There was no salary. I told Ellie who would have summer vacation from her teaching position and whose salary was allocated across the twelve months. She said, "We're going, aren't we!" So off we went to experience incredibly unforgettable events for seven weeks.

Rocksprings, about 1,000 population, called "The Angora Goat Capital of the World," is located in west Texas.

On the way to Rocksprings, we drove through Dallas. It was unbearably hot and humid. Noticing that many cars had their windows rolled up, I said to Ellie, "Do you think it might help?" So we shut our windows. It didn't help. We had not heard of air-conditioned cars!

When we arrived at the parsonage, we discovered that we had been pounded. The cupboard and refrigerator were stacked with a pound of this, a pound of that!

We were invited to dinner one evening. "You can't miss our place. Take the first driveway on the right" After driving 22 miles scrutinizing the shoulder, we found the first driveway. And a bumper gate! Drive up slowly to the double gate with a pole in the middle. Hit the left gate and when it swings open, drive through quickly! A few of the bumper gates were single. Our car was an Edsel with a long back end that took a few whacks before I learned how hard to hit the gas!

Weekly worship services were also held in a schoolhouse forty miles south of Rocksprings in Carta Valley, alternating between a Baptist minister and me. An annual evening week-long revival meeting was also held. As it was the Methodists' turn, they asked me to preach. I gave strong altar calls, but as everyone there was either Baptist or Methodist, there was no response to the call! We spent an overnight on a ranch and watched a goat round-up the next morning. Rocksprings is known as the Angora Goat Capital of the world.

The revival ended with a huge goat barbecue. Delicious! After the meal, they passed the hat. Bill announced, "It's not enough!" The hat was passed again and they gave us $300! So I really did receive a salary!

The same Bill owned the ranch where we stayed. He and Mary also invited us on an overnight trip to Carlsbad Caverns in New Mexico just before we left Rocksprings. Seven years later, they visited us in Minnesota.

On another overnight trip, six of us drove in our Edsel to Monterey, Mexico. It was hot. Ida Mae suggested putting dry ice in the back window. She assured us it would cool us off. It didn't help!

The pastor chose only standard hymns from The Methodist Hymnal for the Rocksprings worship services. As the congregation missed gospel songs, we held a Gospel Sing one Sunday evening. What a rollicking time we had as they shouted out their favorites.

A first for me—another unforgettable—was giving the invocation at the annual 4th of July Rodeo. I didn't know whether to pray for the riders or the animals. As the Rodeo was a big deal with folks coming from all over, the hotel owner panicked because she was short of restaurant help, so Ellie volunteered to waitress. Was she popular! She had been a waitress at the famous Lowell Inn in Stillwater, Minnesota during her high school and college years.

Dear hearts and gentle people live in Rocksprings. We kept in touch with several over the years. Hardin and Gladys visited us in Milaca. Having no children of their own, Hardin was thrilled and proud that it was to him that our first-born, Jack, took his first step.

Marge and her son Jack also visited us, and I took them to a Minnesota Twins baseball game. In 2003, we returned to Rocksprings where we searched and found a Stained Glass Window shop. We went in and asked if this was Jack's business. A woman introduced herself as his wife and asked who we were. A voice from the back of the store called out, "Is that Doug Norris? I recognize his voice!" We found Jack!

The hospitality mat was rolled out. We visited a dear widow who had become a bride while we were there in 1959, worshiped in the church the next morning and were invited to a sumptuous dinner prepared by Jack's wife, Cindy, at their ranch.

Down under

I decided to pursue the Doctor of Ministry degree at San Francisco Theological Seminary in San Anselmo, California. There were cluster study groups in the Manteca area and one summer of course work at the seminary. While at the seminary, I met Les Brockway, a pastor in St. Lucia—a suburb of Brisbane, Queensland, Australia. We became good friends, and I invited him to preach one Sunday in Manteca. One day he told me that the exchange he had worked out with a pastor in England had fallen through and asked if I would consider exchanging with him.

Before I sang, *"I'll go where you want me to go, dear Lord,"* I needed to check with Ellie. While we drove to a Carol Channing performance in Reno to celebrate our 20th wedding anniversary, I simply asked, "Would you like to live in Australia for a few months next year?" Again, she chose adventure and encouraged, "Let's go!"

Off we went in September 1979 for four months with Jack, who delayed university for a year, and Craig, who joined 7th graders for their final quarter of the school year. Tim elected to stay in Manteca to play football. He stayed with wonderful church friends and joined us at

152

Thanksgiving. My parents flew from Phoenix, joined Tim in Honolulu and accompanied him to Australia.

Les and I exchanged congregations, houses and cars but kept our own salaries. What a glorious, unforgettable adventure we had! The Aussies in our churches were happy, friendly, faithful disciples. I was pastor of two churches—one formerly Presbyterian (Swann Road Church) and one formerly Methodist (Ryans Road Church). The denominations (along with the Congregational) had recently merged into The Uniting Church of Australia. There were two morning services, one in each church, and a Sunday evening service in the Presbyterian church. We lived in the Presbyterian manse.

Kookaburra

On our first Sunday, I walked to Swann Road Church early to pray and run through the sermon. Suddenly, I was startled by loud, raucous laughter. I went outside to see nothing. When I went home, I told Ellie about the kids who had the loudest laugh. Later, I learned about the kookaburra, the laughing bird. Oh, how they laugh!

Toowoomba

One of the first Saturdays, we drove to Toowoomba and beyond, a round trip of 200 miles. When I told the congregations the next day, they gasped, "You went that far?" They were incredulous, because not only was the way to Toowoomba a two-lane road, the road beyond was one lane where, when meeting a car, only two wheels could remain on the pavement! It was a long day! I told them we wanted to see the outback. They laughed, and one of them drove us to a vacant lot and said, "There's the outback!"

The following Saturday we again visited Toowoomba, the Garden City—anxious to see the Carnival of Flowers where we were unbelievably awed by the transformation of what we would call lawns into fairylands of blooming flowers, shrubs, walkways, and waterfalls to create illusions we still remember.

Excursions

When the congregations realized we really wanted to see the sights, folks began inviting us for Saturday excursions. Only later did we learn that it was all organized! One Saturday the congregations rented a bus and away we went to the Glasshouse Mountains enjoying views of Mt. Cootha, sugar cane fields, tour of the ginger factory and crystallized ginger candy at Buderim on Queensland's Sunshine Coast. We also rode a train through the Sunshine Plantation and saw fruits, macadamia nuts, pineapples and vegetables.

Another day we had fun at Lone Pine Sanctuary, where we held a koala bear cub and admired kangaroos, colorful lorakeets, cockatoos and the platypus.

*　　*　　*

When the doorbell rang one morning, we expected to greet our hosts. Surprise! Smiling at us were Mick and Lorena from Manteca Church. Harold and Carol invited them to join us for an excursion and picnic. Mick had served under General MacArthur in Australia during World War II. Mick and Harold, a harbor pilot, became good friends sharing memories.

A few years later when Harold and Carol visited us in Manteca, we invited Mick and Lorena to join us all for a long day trip to Yosemite Park. We had a wonderful time. Harold was sitting next to me in the co-pilot seat when we came to a four-way stop. As I waited my turn, Harold was amazed. He exclaimed, "In Australia, horns would be honking with drivers vying to go first." I explained that we take turns; when two cars arrive simultaneously, the one on the right goes first. He shook his head.

*   *   *

We met my folks and Tim in Sydney just before Thanksgiving (which is not celebrated in Australia). As Les's car seated only four people, we rented a second car which Jack drove, following us on the two-day trip south to Sydney. We toured Sydney, drove west to Canberra the capital, and north to Invernell, the site of a recently completed state-of-the-art dam which had been engineered by the uncle of the twins I will write about later. Some years later we reconnected when David and his parents visited us in Palo Alto.

The flies in rural Australia are unbelievable. They swarmed around our faces, and we could understand why Aussies wear hats with strings suspended from the brims. My parents were amazed by the flies and intrigued with

Australia. My Dad carried a small notebook in which he wrote unusual phrases and kept a journal.

My Dad's favorite pie was mince pie. When he saw a menu item at an outside stand called "mincemeat pie," he ordered it. We tried to tell him it was not what he was expecting, but he ordered it anyway, took a bite, spit it out on the ground and exclaimed "What the h... is that!" Aussie pies are hand-held crusts filled with ground beef.

The Swann Road Church held a rummage sale, but they called it "Trash and Treasure," a much better title. Ellie joined the workers, sorting, organizing the items, arranging, cleaning, pricing, selling, and buying a few things for us. She won their hearts! Years later in their letters, some were still fondly remembering Ellie's enthusiastic participation.

Christmas

When I asked how they celebrated Christmas, they had blank looks on their faces. As you know, Christmas in American churches is royally celebrated. I said, "No dinner? No Sunday School program? No Christmas Eve service?" For my benefit, they did host a festive dinner early in December, but by the time Christmas came, I realized why there was no activity. The hot, humid weather is unbelievable. They did have a 7:00 am service on Christmas Day, then many gathered their gifts, lunch, a small plastic Christmas tree and headed for the beach. We joined the Orford family and had a grand time, especially the boys when we walked by a topless sun bather!

Back home

When we returned to Manteca, we found the exchange had been very successful. The congregation loved the Brockways and responded well to Les' ministry. The senior high youth group, however, had fallen apart but our son Tim took charge and soon had the youth returning and the youth ministry thriving. Throughout our ministry, our three sons saw themselves as important participants and supporters.

On reflection, I decided I didn't have the time to research and write a dissertation for the Doctor of Ministry degree. The Australia experience seemed an incomparable educational substitute.

A month after we returned, Les was called to an Aboriginal school and church in northwestern Australia. The Orfords, representing Swann Road and Ryans Road Churches, telephoned to ask me to return and become their permanent pastor. We were tempted, but decided it was important for our sons to complete their education in America.

Three years later after another pastoral change, we were visited by the Skermans who again asked me to become their permanent pastor. But this time I was being transferred as well. They wished us well.

Lasting friendships were formed with the good folks of St. Lucia. Several have visited us and we correspond regularly.

The Holy Land

In 1988, we led a tour of Israel, Jordan and Egypt—a 21-day trip. Landing in Jordan, Ellie and the group visited Petra (I was ill!) and then we boarded a bus for Israel. What an unforgettable experience touring the Galilee region, Caesarea, Mt. Carmel, Jerusalem, Dead Sea and Masada.

The tour bus stopped on a hill overlooking Jerusalem and I sang *"The Holy City."* According to one woman who wrote me a thank you note, there wasn't a dry eye in the bus! We then went to Egypt by bus with an overnight at Mt. Sinai which we climbed! We were scheduled to reach the top to see the sunrise, but our guide took us the "short" but steep way, not realizing how slow our group climbed. Needless to say, we missed the sunrise, and our guide was not very popular! Amid the accumulated trash left by previous inconsiderate visitors, we held a short service, thanking God for the privilege to be in this holy place where Moses received the Ten Commandments.

In Egypt, we marveled at the pyramids and the Nile. We went up the river to Luxor by overnight train (a very uncomfortable trip) and returned to Cairo by boat.

We were accompanied by Dr. Robert Hamerton-Kelly who was Dean of the Stanford Chapel. He lectured at the sites we visited, along with the local guides. At Armageddon, he told the history, rather than the radical, scary fundamentalist version of the future. The Israeli guide was astonished, "You should hear some of the hair curling talks that have been given here!"

Bob also arranged for a private tour of what is believed to be the actual site of the crucifixion, far below the present floor of the Church of the Holy Sepulcher. It was a very moving experience as we sang, *"Were You There When They Crucified My Lord?"*

Europe

In 1990, I was granted a 10-week Study Leave. The theme of the sabbatical was learning How Churches Relate to Their Culture—how they survive, how they reach out to their communities. We interviewed church leaders in Northern Ireland, East Germany, West Germany and Czechoslovakia.

The institutional church in Northern Ireland was relatively insulated from the tumultuous relationship between Catholics and Protestants. One Methodist pastor flatly stated, *"We Prods (Protestants) were not interested in what went on outside our doors."* One Presbyterian pastor tried. As the early immigrants to Ireland were from Scotland, the Presbyterian Church is dominant. The minister apologized to a Catholic Church for a bombing. He made friends with the priest and encouraged interfaith services. The result? He was forced by his elders to resign.

So what did God do? God went outside the institutional church. We visited three Reconciliation Centers in Northern Ireland staffed by both Protestants and Catholics—Rostrevor, Cornerstone, Corrymeela—centers which were signs of hope in that troubled land.

We spent three weeks in Ireland—one week in a cottage on Galway Bay and one week in Northern Ireland, Belfast in particular, where there were multiple check points staffed by police in armored tanks.

We had made housing arrangements for three of the ten weeks; the rest of the time we found Bed and Breakfasts wherever we happened to be. There was only one night when we almost had to sleep in the car. Usually we stopped at a B&B about 5:00, but one night in western Ireland we had problems. There was a bank holiday and "No Vacancies" abounded. Finally, at 8:00 just as the receptionist was shaking her head "No," a cancellation was called in!

*   *   *

In the former Communist countries, we were humbled and inspired to hear stories of how Christians dealt with discrimination, yet kept the faith. Christians were denied promotions and even jobs. Children of pastors were not admitted to the universities. One pastor told us of a ten-year old boy who, at least once a week, was called to the principal's office (remember how intimidating it is to be called to the principal's office) to explain why he had not joined the Communist youth movement. We were told of a pastor in Yugoslavia who, 15 years before, requested a raise in salary as they were expecting a baby. (Salaries were paid by the government.) The request was sent to a local authority who investigated and concluded he was being paid too much, so they lowered his salary!

Harry, a United Methodist layperson who lived in East Berlin, told us that the Berlin wall, erected almost overnight, was completed on August 13, 1959. Until the wall fell, Harry fasted every August 13. His son was forced to leave East Germany in 1972. When the wall fell in 1989, their Christmas celebration was the first time in 18 years the entire family gathered together. Although many East Germans are bitter, blaming the Socialists for taking 40 years of their lives, Harry said, "But I'm not bitter. They took my money, they took my freedom, they took my son, but not my life. I would not let them."

In contrast to the insulated churches of Northern Ireland, East Berlin churches played a significant role Before the Wall and After the Wall. As churches were the only place where people could meet without permission, they facilitated Round Tables where communists, farmers, laborers, white collar workers and professionals could come together and talk. People did not come to worship in large numbers, but they did come to the Round Tables. Actually, Roman Catholic, Lutheran and Methodist churches taught parliamentary procedures to the new democracy. In fact, After the Wall, Round Tables governed until elections were held. Its participants became leaders because they had learned how to think, speak in public, and conduct meetings.

Ten years before the wall fell, prayer services were begun. An annual Peace Conference was organized. Some credit prayer for bringing the wall down.

The stance of the church Before the Wall was stated by the Lutheran Bishop of East Berlin: "Be Christians within Socialism." The church attempted not to be **for** or **against** Socialism, but to be the church *in* Socialism. The Catholic Church backed off and raised no protests, but the Protestant churches continued its opposition to military instruction in schools, maintained its confirmation program and sought an alternative to military service.

*   *   *

Ellie and I arrived in Berlin six weeks after the wall fell. What an unforgettable experience! The contrast between West and East Germany was stark. East Berlin was depressing. The feeling of oppression was vivid. The city was bleak, laden with heavy smog. The apartment buildings were architecturally ugly, built for function, not beauty, and badly in need of paint and repair. The cheaply made autos belched black, dirty exhaust. In stark contrast, West Berlin was clean, sparkling and modern. The walk through Checkpoint Charlie was emotional.

We spent three weeks in Germany with a side trip to Denmark and Sweden to escape the smog and heat of East Berlin, one week in Czechoslovakia (it had not yet divided into Slovakia and the Czech Republic) and one week in Dartmouth, England.

On our quick weekend side-trip to Sweden, we were hosted by Ellie's relatives. We worshiped at the Lutheran Church where her grandfather was baptized, and we saw the family farm. We also visited the archive museum in

Vexjo where Ellie found a record of her mother's 1902 baptism in Scandia, Minnesota!

In Bratislava, we met the Methodist pastor and his wife. After an afternoon interview, we invited them to dinner.

Prague was special as it has not been bombed in any war. We stayed a few nights in a hostel at a Methodist Church and were especially blessed by the friendship of the pastor and his wife who prepared breakfast. We also enjoyed the countryside when we took them on a drive to see his other church two hours away

Czechoslovakians have an indomitable spirit that eventually brought down the Communist regime. In November 1989, on Wenceslas Square in Prague, students demonstrated peacefully by keeping a candle vigil day and night. Their weapons were candles. At night the demonstrators, holding candles, faced a barricade of armed policemen. The leaders of the Communist Party resigned. A mound of candle wax in the square serves as a sobering reminder of the cost and value of freedom.

Our final week of my study leave was enjoyed in Dartmouth, England (the mouth of the River Dart.) Our apartment was located downtown over an antique shop. We discovered, by reading the guest book written in by former tenants, that our job was to wind the clock that looked out over the town.

We also were interested to learn some Pilgrim history. After leaving Southampton, the Mayflower and her sister ship, the Speedwell, set off. But the Speedwell began taking on water (some stories suggest the crew deliberately sabotaged her to get out of their long contracts). So the two ships pulled into Dartmouth for repairs. While repairs were undertaken, the ships sheltered in Bayard's Cove on the River Dart which at that time was Dartmouth's only harbor. The seawalls and riverfront probably looked much the same as they do now and a few of the houses, which date from the 17th century, may also have been standing then.

Recalling my connection with the Pilgrims was a delightful way to end our unbelievable and unforgettable ten weeks in Europe, The Norris family traces our ancestors back to the Mayflower. Granddaughter Adrienne, while a fifth grader, began a speech with "April showers bring May flowers. What do Mayflowers bring? My ancestors!" Tradition tells us that 13-year old Mary Chilton (our ancestor) was the first to step on Plymouth Rock.

*   *   *

We saw walls: rock walls in Ireland to mark boundaries (walls made from rocks that were removed so they could farm); walls that were built to keep Jews in the internment camps (we visited Buchenwald and Dacchau—unbelievably horrible!); the Berlin wall was erected almost overnight to keep people in, not to keep people out; and walls in Belfast were built to keep people apart!

We met Christians who lived their lives walled in, but with faith, courage and hope, they waited and worked for the destruction of walls and the construction of community.

I'll go . . . to the Holy Land again!

In 1995, it was again my privilege to tour Israel, thanks to Palo Alto Church friends Ed and Erletta who, as active members of the Masonic and Eastern Star lodges, sponsored me for an escorted seven-day trip for pastors under the auspices of Knights Templar. In addition to the sites I had visited on my previous trip, we took a ride on a replica of a first century boat which had been discovered and excavated only six years before. I planted trees in honor of Ed, Erletta and Merced Church and presented them with certificates when I returned home. Planting trees to restore the forests is a sign of hope. A highlight of the week was an evening session with a Palestinian, educated in the United States, who shared the Palestinian perspective on the Israeli-Arab conflict.

CHAPTER TWENTY

Jesus Said, "Go . . . Heal the Sick"

Jesus was well known and popular for his healings and, subsequently, ministering to the sick is an important ministry of the church. In recent years, the church has reclaimed the importance of healing prayers, healing services and anointing with oil.

*   *   *

The smallest babies born in Australia were grandchildren of Charles and Joy Jones of the Ryans Road Church. When we arrived in Australia, they were a few days old. We have photos of the twin boys, each of them being held in the palm of a nurse's hand. When they were released from the hospital in late December, I was asked to anoint them and conduct a healing service for the boy who had a serious eye complication. The twins survived and are now strapping adults.

Parking lot healing

Several of us gathered in the sanctuary on a Tuesday morning for prayers of praise to rejoice with Mary who had just come from the doctor with tremendous news—a CT scan revealed there were no longer any signs of cancer. A friend began bringing Mary to church several months previously. Fighting cancer, Mary was feeling the need for spiritual help. Her friend Jean, an Easter worshiper (!) told Mary, "Let me take you to a neat church!" They started coming regularly. One Sunday they put in a prayer request, and we prayed for Mary in the Sunday morning service.

Several weeks later, we "remembered our baptism" during the worship service. We pastors walked through the congregation sprinkling water on the congregation and saying, "Remember your baptism." A few drops of water touched Mary on her hand, and she felt them like a sting. After the service, as she was getting into her car in the parking lot, she suddenly was zapped with a bright light. It surrounded and filled her. Her friend Jean didn't see the light, but she knew something was happening because Mary almost fell over backward.

The next Sunday they came to our Healing Service and Mary told us of her experience. She said she felt so clean. We laid hands on Mary and prayed for her healing. Tuesday, the CT scan showed no signs of cancer anywhere. Mary rejoices in the joy and wonder of the cleansing spiritual healing experience that occurred in the church parking lot!

*   *   *

"May I pray with you?" I asked a church member who was in the hospital. Startled, he replied, "Am I that sick?" I wonder if he had confused Last Rites with a prayer for healing.

*   *   *

The Japanese pastors with whom I worked in Wesley Church sang with patients, especially those who were terminally ill. I was then retired with years of ministry behind me and I wish I had realized how singing hymns are comforting and healing. Many hospitals now offer live music—vocal and harp—to comfort their patients.

Chapter Twenty-One

"Extend Hospitality to Strangers"
(Romans 12.31)

The Robinsons

Through the years, we have been overwhelmed with hospitality, showered with generous acts of unrequited hospitality by people of our congregations. In addition, one incident is particularly memorable.

I was asked to conduct a funeral on Christmas Eve afternoon, and the family was so grateful I was given a $100 honorarium, which was a lot of money in 1970! Surprised, I went home and said to Ellie, "Let's go to the Rose Bowl!" Stanford was playing for the first time in twenty years, and as we had family season tickets (which allowed us to sit behind the goal posts in open seating), we were eligible to purchase two tickets. We looked in the newspaper want ads and found one more ticket for sale, which allowed Jack, Tim and me to go to the game.

Excitedly we drove to Pasadena. This was our first time on Hwy 101 (there was no I-5), and when we drove through Santa Barbara I was mesmerized by the scenic beauty, until a police siren pulled us over, and I was given a $25 ticket for speeding! There went ¼ of my $100 honorarium!

On New Year's Eve Day, we had fun touring Universal Studios. On New Year's Day, by the time we reached the parade route, even though we got up at 4:30, there were so many people we could only sit on a curb looking at the back end of the floats and bands as they went by!

Following the parade, I drove through Rose Bowl Stadium neighborhoods and eventually parked on a street in a residential area, right next to a school and playground where Ellie could keep 3½-year old Craig entertained while the other two boys and I went to the game.

We had two seats together, and one seat in another part of the stadium, so one boy sat with me for half the game and then switched with his brother for the other half. Can you imagine 8-year old Tim sitting by himself! Never would we allow that today! But, Tim was so thrilled to be at a Stanford Rose Bowl game; he had no fear. Jack was ten at the time.

While we were at the game, a woman came out of her home, crossed the street to the playground and asked Ellie, "Is your family at the game?" She introduced herself as Mrs. Robinson and then invited Ellie to come to her house to watch the game and Craig to play with their two sons. She asked Ellie, "Do you know of Jackie Robinson? He is my husband's brother." Ellie enjoyed watching the game and visiting with Mack Robinson! And Ellie learned that Mrs. Robinson, released from the hospital only that morning, was recovering from surgery. Now, that is hospitality!

After the game, Mack insisted that Ellie and Craig not return to the car, but wait until we returned. He wanted to meet us. Then he insisted that he drive his car and lead us on a shortcut to the freeway to avoid the heavy traffic. Our last image was Mack waving with a big smile on his face and pointing to the entrance ramp.

When we drove down the grapevine into the San Joaquin Valley, we hit Tule fog which slowed us down considerably. I was so tired Ellie and I took turns driving. When she drove, I lay down in the back seat on the floor over the hump. The boys were on the seat. But, we had to get home for church. I wasn't preaching but I had other tasks. What an unforgettable trip!

Coley

He stopped by the Manteca church office two or three times a week. Not staying long, he wanted to check in and share a thought, usually ending by repeating some of the same stories.

He had a lot of guilt to work through. Coley was a retired Marine of the old school. He treated his son as if he were a Marine, or would someday be a Marine. Coley was tough, demanding and unaffectionate.

Philip enlisted in the Marines and when he left home for duty asked his father, "Will you do something for me?"

Gruffly as usual, Coley asked, "What?"

"I want you to start going to my church."

"Where is that?"

"St. Paul's."

Philip was killed in action, and Coley, filled with grief over the might-have-beens, never missed a Sunday, and frequently stopped by the office, honoring (in my opinion) his son.

Raised a Southern Baptist, he would tease, "The Bible says John the Baptist, not John the Methodist!" I soon started saying, "John the Baptizer"!

Coley was not morose, but animated, energetic and enthusiastic. His neighbor said to him one day, "How come you are always so peppy?" Coley replied, "Why, I reverse the numbers. I'm 73, but I feel like I'm 37!" The neighbor moaned, "Just my luck—I'm 69!"

One day Coley brought me a large, beautiful maple tree leaf he had found. I admired it, pointed to my desk, and said, "Leaf it there." He laughed about that for weeks and had it framed. We still have it.

While Coley stopped by the church, Blanche, alone and lonely, stopped by the parsonage two or three times a week to visit with Ellie.

Downtown

Hospitality is an important ministry of a downtown church where there are many persons with special emotional and mental needs. Palo Alto church had its share, and I tried to spend time with each one. They were all lonely and appreciated finding a place where they felt they belonged and were appreciated. Some were given tasks to do, but most wanted to be listened to and helped with their problems. John was epileptic, Ruthea and her child were homeless, Bernice was a WW II veteran with special needs and no family.

Dorothy came every day, riding the bus all the way from San Jose. She walked the halls, up and down, taxing the patience of the office staff. She constantly wanted to visit with me, so I made a daily appointment with her, offered her coffee and talked for ten minutes or so. She walked the halls, reminding the staff about her appointment!

Palo Alto Church was also a strong supporter of The Urban Ministry to the homeless. And, one week a month, the church provided overnight shelter and meals in the church building.

Cuppa coffee?

Learning from the Palo Alto staff's daily 10:00 coffee break, I invited Barbara, the Merced Church Administrative Assistant, to join me for a daily break. Barbara had quickly understood my instruction that her primary responsibility was ministry, with business matters taking second. I told her, "If we don't have a bulletin on Sunday, so be it." On the phone or in person, she understood that she was engaged in ministry, and soon realized that persons with church business often had a deeper personal agenda. She even prayed with people over the phone.

So, Barbara began inviting retired men to join our coffee break. Sometimes wives came, but most of the time it was men. Besides bars, where do retired men go to "hang out"? The word spread and some days there were 25 of us gathered to drink coffee, share stories, and offer support to one another. Some stayed afterwards and did odd jobs. Pastries were often shared, and we even celebrated birthdays.

CHAPTER TWENTY-TWO

"Bless Me Too, My Father"

(Genesis 27:38)

A plaintive, poignant, heart-rending plea was made by Esau to his father Isaac, *"Have you but one blessing, my father? Bless me too, O my father."* And then, *"Esau lifted up his voice and wept."* His twin brother, Jacob, had stolen the blessing that was Esau's. For children in biblical times, receiving the Blessing was a momentous event. It gave the children a tremendous sense of being highly valued by their parents. At a specific time in their lives they would hear words of encouragement, love and acceptance from their parents. Traditional Jewish homes, through the centuries, and even yet today, bestow a blessing on their children.

Jesus blessed the children; *"Jesus hugged the children and blessed them."* (Mark 13:16)

* * *

I am indebted to the book, *The Blessing*, by Gary Smalley and John Trent as it gives a fresh perspective on family relationships based on the biblical Blessing.

"No matter your age, the approval of your parents affects how you view yourself and your ability to pass that approval along to your children, spouse, and friends. Many

people spend a lifetime looking for this acceptance the Bible calls The Blessing. . . . All of us long to be accepted by others. While we may say out loud, "I don't care what other people think about me," on the inside we all yearn for intimacy and affection. This yearning is especially true in our relationship with our parents. Gaining or missing out on parental approval has a tremendous effect on us, even if it has been years since we have had any regular contact with them. In fact, what happens in our relationship with our parents can greatly affect all our present and future relationships.

*   *   *

Elizabeth O'Connor of the Church of the Saviour in Washington, D. C., wrote *Cry Pain, Cry Hope* in which she discusses the Blessing. She says that we each need the Blessing in order to be set free, free of the nest, free of the dependency on our parents, free to live our lives. (pp. 48-51)

"We need the blessing of each other to be set free. The parent who has blessed the child leaves that child free to run toward life. The parent who has withheld his or her blessing binds the child in intractable ways. The blessing is integral to the experiencing of our separateness—to being our own persons and going our own ways. . . . Perhaps those who clutch the most and who block our way never felt blessed themselves. . . . Yearning for the blessing never given can keep us forever fixed in the past, forever wanting

178

what was withheld, forever looking to authority figures and significant others for the benediction a parent never gave."

The good news of the gospel is that those who have not received the blessing can overcome, can have a second chance, by receiving the Blessing from God within the context of the church family where we bless each other, and by giving the blessing to the parent who did not give it.

I have preached sermons and conducted workshops on the blessing. Bless your children and grandchildren by touching (hugging) them, telling them, "I love you," and expressing their high value and your hope for their future. If it is impossible to touch and bless them personally, write a letter. In his final days, knowing he would soon die, Ellie's Dad wrote beautiful letters of blessing to our three boys and to me. Ellie and I have tried to write notes of thanks and blessings to our children and grandchildren on their birthdays, and they in turn write to us.

*   *   *

I'll never forget the Blessing my maternal grandfather Irwin gave me. I was in seminary, some 400 miles from home, when he was dying of cancer.

A few weeks prior to his death, we drove home for my sister's wedding. I can still vividly see "Pop" sitting in his chair, aching with pain. As I was returning to Illinois, we both knew we probably would never see each other again. I was given the beautiful gift of being able to say "goodbye," and he in turn blessed me. Neither of us knew it was a blessing; our culture has not taught us to give blessings.

But he took my hands, told me how proud he was of me, and that he knew I would do good in this world. I'll never forget his Blessing. It has sustained me when I have doubted my abilities, and encouraged me when I've been discouraged. You see, I know my grandfather believed in me. I am not just sure, or hope, I know. I know because he told me.

Don't assume people around you know how you feel about them. Don't assume, because none of us are mind readers. My grandfather told me, and I'll never forget his pride in me, his belief in my high value, and his picture of my future in which I would do good in this world.

*   *   *

How I was unbelievably blessed on my 50th birthday! It was Easter Sunday, and I had returned to Palo Alto Church, this time as Senior Pastor. I was surprised by being serenaded by 1,000 people in two services, accompanied by a 40-piece orchestra, singing "Happy Birthday."

*   *   *

Active church members, we knew them both well. The daughter sat by her mother's bed. The mother with labored, heavy gasps was obviously very uncomfortable. Her daughter said she had been struggling for two days. Ellie and I had been out of town and hearing the daughter's message on our phone, we went to the hospital immediately. Putting my hand on the mother's forehead and saying her name, I gave her the traditional blessing which I give to those who are dying: *"The Lord bless you and keep you. The Lord make his face to shine upon you. The Lord lift up the light of his countenance upon you, and give you peace now and forevermore."* The daughter told me later that we probably were still in the hospital when her mother stopped breathing and died. Her mother had been married to a pastor. I did not realize that the blessing I gave her was the one he used to conclude worship services. When she heard the familiar blessing, she may have felt permission to let go.

Golden wedding anniversary

Ellie and I celebrated our 50th wedding anniversary by being overwhelmed with blessings. On Saturday August 15, 2008 our family hosted a grand reception for 300 people at the Palo Alto Church including a surprise Renewal of Vows ceremony conducted by Bob Schwartz, a friend and colleague. Our eight grandchildren walked down the aisle, each carrying a rose that became Ellie's bouquet. Ellie walked down the aisle on her brother's arm. His appearance was a complete surprise as he had told Ellie, much to her disappointment, that he couldn't come.

On Sunday, August 16, at Wesley Church (the actual date of our anniversary), I invited Family Campers to come, sing, and enjoy the celebration. Wesley Church has the beautiful custom of having a few words spoken describing the person/s for whom the chancel flowers are dedicated, followed by a favorite hymn or song of the honoree/s. Shirley gave the flowers that Sunday in honor of our anniversary. Craig started to play *"The Old Gray Mare She Ain't What She Used to Be,"* but quickly switched to one of Ellie's favorites—*"Imagine."*

After the service, the church hosted one of their famous potlucks followed by a delightful humorous program, which included a mock renewal of vows and music by the Ukulele Choir.

Go . . . to Emmaus

"We would like you to Walk to Emmaus." I sang, "I'll go . . ." No, not a physical, literal walk to the village of Emmaus, three miles from Jerusalem, but a three-day spiritual walk, overflowing with blessings. Ed and Georgianna from Ohio were staying in Palo Alto while Ed, a heart surgeon, did advanced work at Stanford. They sent me to Wilmington, Ohio, and Ellie to Fresno, California where we both experienced the Walk. The Walk to Emmaus, designed and distributed by Upper Room publications, is based on the Roman Catholic Cursillo. The purpose is to renew the church by developing Christian leaders and disciples.

Both of us were abundantly blessed by the experience and we returned to Palo Alto to help Ed and Georgianna bring the movement to northern California. The first walks were held in the Palo Alto church and soon spread across the conference.

After we moved to Merced, we were encouraged to hold the first Chrysalis in the church buildings. Chrysalis is the youth version of the Walk. Subsequent walks were and are being held in the church buildings.

At the Boys' Chrysalis one weekend, one of the tables invented the name, "Spiritually Challenged." Their logo was a cross on a wheelchair. However, at the end of the weekend, one of the boys said, "We are no longer spiritually challenged!" Amen

A teen-ager told his story. His life was godless and hopeless. One evening, the black hole of despair so overwhelmed him that he took a razor blade and slashed his wrist and arm 15 times! Psychiatric treatment helped him out of his hopeless depression, but he still suffered the black hole of despair. Then he attended a Boys' Chrysalis. With tears streaming down his face, he knelt in the Merced Church sanctuary and gave the Lord his despair. God heard his prayer, lifted his heavy burden and filled him with the love of Christ. God is good!

*   *   *

I had a profound spiritual experience on one of the walks. We were in the process of moving from Palo Alto to Merced and I was the Spiritual Director of a Women's Walk to Emmaus. Friday evening, through a guided meditation led by another pastor, we were invited to visualize Jesus and ask him two questions. After the group returned to the conference room, I went to the altar and wept. The tears just flowed. I asked two questions, "Will leaving Palo Alto be smooth, considering all the logistics, decisions, and farewells?" My second question was, "What will happen in Merced?" Merced Church was going through a crisis. The congregation was very angry with the bishop, and I was being sent to reconcile! I had a lot of apprehension and anxiety.

While I knelt at the altar that evening praying and weeping, the assurance came to me that leaving Palo Alto would be smooth, that everything would work out. But no answer came to my Merced question. The next morning I gave a talk. During intermission, Marion told me that while I was speaking she saw an aura around me—a brilliant, white light. Then the Holy Spirit filled her from head to toe, flooding her with the message, "Tell Doug he will have a wonderful ministry in Merced." She gave me the answer to my second question!

*   *   *

"Bless me" was Esau's plaintive cry, echoed by many who yearn to know, who need to know they are loved, who need to be blessed by parents, loved ones and God. In Merced Church each Sunday following the sermon, I extended an invitation to come forward, kneel at the altar rail to be blessed—to receive Jesus as Lord and Savior and to be blessed on birthdays, anniversaries and for special needs.

CHAPTER TWENTY-THREE

Wedding Memories

Everybody loves weddings—weddings are festive, memorable and filled with hope, and love abounds! From childhood, young girls dream of a fairyland wedding as the prelude to "And they lived happily ever after." During premarital counseling sessions, when the groom made a suggestion for the wedding service, I would interrupt. "She and her mother have been planning this wedding since she was a little girl. It's nice you can be there but keep your opinions to yourself." It was said with humor, but he usually got the point.

Even when it requires a financial sacrifice, proud parents want to do the very best to help their daughter fulfill her dream.

Wedding celebrations have changed dramatically through the decades. In the early years of my ministry in rural Minnesota, attendants included a Maid of Honor, bridesmaid, flower girl, perhaps a ring bearer, Best Man and an usher or two. The receptions were usually held in the church basement or a local hall. Beverages were coffee, tea and punch with a beautifully decorated wedding cake, along with mints and nuts, producing oohs and ahhs.

How weddings have changed! Now elaborate receptions with banquet meals, champagne, open bars and dancing are held in country clubs or gardens. But still the cake is central.

Regardless of the size or venue, all weddings are special and it was always my joy to officiate in celebration of a new marriage.

Every pastor has wedding stories to tell. Here are some of mine.

*   *   *

Beginning with ours! The time to gather at the church came and went. My family and I had not arrived. Imagine the anxiety as Ellie and her wedding party speculated about what might have happened. Car trouble? An accident? Forgot something? (This was years before cellphones.) Finally, 45 minutes behind schedule, we arrived. My parents, sister and I, looking for a shortcut so we wouldn't be late, ended up in a pasture somewhere! With a sigh of relief, the beautiful wedding went off without a hitch, except we tried to tape the service but, inadvertently, put the reel to reel tape recorder next to a fan.

*   *   *

The organist had begun playing the prelude. It was time to start the "Wedding March." The Wedding Hostess was nervous. I was concerned. Finally, a mother rushed in holding a gown she had just finished sewing for her daughter who was a bridesmaid.

*   *   *

Palo Alto Church's sanctuary was especially popular with Chinese couples. I was happy to officiate and we soon learned and resigned ourselves to admit the wedding would not start until at least an hour after the scheduled time. Evidently it was traditional.

*   *   *

Before the wedding started, the professional photographer gasped. His camera malfunctioned, and the professional photographer had not brought a spare. The bride's fairlyland wedding had no professional photos. Notice how I keep repeating "professional"?

*   *   *

Because of a sizzling heat wave, I strongly urged the bride not to have the receiving line at the church. "It's too hot," but she insisted. So 300 people stood in line on a hot summer afternoon in the church with no air-conditioning. At the country club, the table with the guest list was located just inside the country club door, so 300 people stood in line in the hot sun in the parking lot waiting to write their names. Once inside, 300 people stood in the buffet line and, yes, there was only one line! "What did you do at the wedding?" "Stood in line."

"We are short of funds. Is there any way you can help us out?" So I waived the church fee and the pastor's fee. Standing with the groom and his party waiting for the wedding music to start, I asked him how they were celebrating their honeymoon. "We're going to Hawaii," he answered proudly. That was the last time I gave a good deal!

*   *   *

And then there were those couples who, I strongly suspect, joined the church because fees for church members were lower. Yes, we never saw them in church again.

*   *   *

Two saints of the church—a widow and a widower—in their 80s announced their intention to marry. When they met with me, they were slightly nervous so I asked "Is this a shotgun wedding?" They laughed and relaxed.

*   *   *

When young women telephoned and excitedly, but nervously, asked if they could be married in our church, I asked, "Do you have a fella?" "Oh, yes!" they giggled.

*   *   *

And there was the wedding when I tried to marry the bride to the Best Man. He was the groom's brother and they

188

both had similar names. That embarrassment brought down the house.

*　　*　　*

At oldest son Jack and Jennifer's wedding, when I asked the Best Man for the ring, he slapped his pockets, looked at the man next to him who slapped his pockets and looked at the man next to him, etc. Finally, the groomsman at the end of the line produced the ring and it was handed up the line to the Best Man. I asked Jack, "Is he the best man you could find?" Oh, how the congregation laughed.

*　　*　　*

The Best Man was the bride's teenage younger brother. When I asked him for the ring, he searched his pockets but couldn't find it. He was frantic so I calmly said, "It's okay; we'll use mine." After the wedding they searched vigorously for the ring and finally found it in a handbell ringer's glove. Bored with nothing better to do, the Best Man, wearing the ring, had been trying on the gloves!

*　　*　　*

The wedding and reception were held at the country club. The groom and all his groomsmen were graduates of the University of Kentucky. The national basketball finals were being televised with Kentucky favored to win. The men gathered in front of the lobby TV captivated by the nail biting close game. We kept stalling the Wedding

Hostess until she insisted that the wedding must begin. With minutes to go, the men reluctantly left the TV and went outside to the garden for the ceremony. At the reception, we learned that Kentucky had lost. What a downer that would have been for the wedding party if they had known the outcome.

*   *   *

Previously I wrote about the "thorn in my flesh," namely my sinus condition. During one wedding in an unfamiliar hall, my "thorn" raised its ugly head. I started coughing and couldn't stop. Leaving the bride and groom, I searched for a drink of water. For years they laughingly told friends how the pastor left them at the altar.

*   *   *

This reminds me of my first Christmas Eve in Merced when, during the sermon, I again got a coughing spell. I left the pulpit, went next door to the pastor's study, found a lozenge in the drawer and told the congregation a previous pastor had generously left me an unused lozenge. Oh, how they laughed.

*   *   *

The bride and her mother, who had been church friends for years, came to the church to finalize some arrangements a few days before the wedding. As we talked, the bride said she was having a chocolate wedding cake. I exclaimed,

"Chocolate! Wedding cakes have to be white; it's in the Bible." Her mother quickly retorted, "At this point, it is easier to change pastors than wedding cakes."

*   *   *

The wedding was held outdoors in the Santa Cruz Mountains. After the service, I noticed a table loaded with pot. My policy: Don't ask, don't tell.

*   *   *

I sometimes blessed the couple: "May there be JOY in your marriage. Let J stand for Jesus, O for others and Y for you. Put Jesus first, your spouse second, and you third and there will be joy. When each of you commits yourself and your marriage to Jesus, and puts the needs of the other first in priority, both of you are winners."

CHAPTER TWENTY-FOUR

If Only

On April 15, 2012, following a delightful, restful cruise to Hawaii, on our way back from San Diego to our home in Mesa, AZ, on I-8, I caught myself nodding and over-corrected. The car went across the freeway, bounced off the mountainside and ended up in the left lane facing the way we had come. Thank God there were no cars near us at the time. I couldn't rouse Ellie and feared she was dead, but then "angels" stopped their cars and came to help. Three nurses and a doctor appeared. One of the nurses revived Ellie. A young man got in the back seat and held Ellie's head straight until the ambulance arrived. A nurse retrieved the suitcase that had been thrown out of the trunk and took it to the hospital.

An ambulance took us to El Centro Hospital. My brother Bob and Lois came from San Diego. The Highway Patrolman told Bob that he didn't understand how we were still alive. I was released with bruises; a cut on Ellie's head was stitched and then she was transferred back to San Diego with two fractures in her pelvis. She spent four days in the University of California Hospital and 19 days in a skilled nursing facility for physical therapy. Subsequently, it was discovered that she had two hematoma on the brain.

Our youngest son Craig flew down from San Francisco the evening of the accident. Phil and Kim graciously invited Craig and me to stay in their guest room. Steve and Frona surprised us with a visit to the hospital and generously offered to let me stay in their condo for three weeks while they returned to Manteca. How grateful we are to God for our lives, for friends and their gracious hospitality.

Then I was bombarded with "If Onlys." If only we hadn't had to return an hour to San Diego for a misplaced piece of luggage. If only we had stayed overnight in San Diego. If only I had pulled over to nap in spite of no rest areas. If only we hadn't gone on a cruise. If only we had stayed in Minnesota and not moved to California. If only I hadn't been born! Uncontrolled If Onlys are strangling, overwhelming, paralyzing.

There is an upside to If Onlys if positive steps are taken to prevent the event from happening again. I now pull over and nap when I feel sleepy. But I'm talking about paralyzing guilt, insidious guilt that prevents us from living life fully in the present—persisting, strangling guilt that keeps us looking backward, living in the past rather than the present. The past cannot be changed. Dwelling on If Onlys changes nothing! Let them go!

Do you carry a load of guilt with you? Burdened with If Onlys? If only I had done . . . if only I had said . . . if only I had not done . . . if only I had not said. On and on! Everybody has guilt! Is that too strong? All those who have no guilt, please raise your hands. Be careful—if you raise your hand, you might then have guilt for lying or denying! Denial is the act of burying the If Onlys into the recesses of our minds where they ferment and rot.

We do not handle guilt well. Especially do we have difficulty forgiving ourselves. Conscientious people, good people, respectable people often fail to live up to their own expectations. They are more tolerant of others than they are tolerant of themselves. They can forgive mistakes of others but have difficulty forgiving their own mistakes.

Even Christians have a difficult time with guilt. We of all people should know how to forgive and how to receive forgiveness. The heart of the Christian gospel—the good news—is that God loves us and saves us from ourselves. The good news is that God forgives sins and eradicates guilt.

The gospel says three things about forgiveness. First, we cannot earn it. Second, it is not for sale. And third, in Christ we already have been forgiven. And so it is with guilt. We cannot get rid of guilt by ourselves. We cannot buy ourselves a conscience free of guilt. But Jesus has already given his life for our guilt to be eradicated. That is the Christian good news. Why, therefore, are so many Christians oppressed with guilt? Why are so many not free, joyous, and confidently living in the here and now, rather than dwelling in past If Onlys?

The question is: How is a guilt-ridden person freed from the insidious If Onlys?

First, believe that God is a God of forgiveness and mercy. Believe that God gives second chances and many

195

chances. Believe that Jesus gave his life for your forgiveness and salvation—a relationship with God that is free of guilt.

Second, confess your sins. 1 John 1:9, *"If we confess our sins, God is faithful and just, and will forgive our sins and cleanse us from all unrighteousness."* Cleanse us. Confess. Tell it. Unload the guilt. Name your sin. Name your guilt. Admit it. Sometimes it helps to tell another person, which is biblical. James 5:16, *"Confess your sins to one another, and pray for one another."* Share your burden. Tell your pastor. Tell a trusted friend. Confess your sins.

Third, receive absolution—the assurance that you are forgiven, you are absolved from your guilt.

But there are those who still have a difficult time believing they are forgiven. They need something more tangible, something more graphic to convince them that they are forgiven. In the Old Testament, sins were symbolically laid on a goat and the goat was driven into the wilderness carrying the sins with it. The term "scapegoat" is from this ritual. The goat took the blame and ran into the wilderness. The imagery was powerful. People could actually see the goat running into the wilderness with their sins. There goes my If Onlys, good riddance! But, then, don't let the goat come back with your guilt. There is a hymn, *"Take your burden to the Lord and leave it there."* Don't lay it on the altar, be forgiven for your If Onlys, and then on the way back to your pew decide that you can't live without your old antagonist. Leave it there!

Sometimes the goat or a lamb was sacrificed. Again, the imagery was powerful. They could actually see the lamb who was carrying their If Onlys butchered and burned on the altar, the If Onlys going up in smoke.

Another ancient ritual with a powerful image was the sprinkling of a lamb's blood on the altar and on the garments of the priests to cleanse, to wash away sins and guilt, to wash away the If Onlys.

We need to reclaim the biblical image of blood. Hebrews 9:12, *"Christ entered once for all into the Holy Place, taking not the blood of goats and calves but his own blood, thus securing an eternal redemption."* At the last supper with his disciples, Jesus took the cup of wine, gave it to his disciples and said, (Matthew 26:27-28) *"Drink of it, all of you; for this is my blood of the covenant, which is poured out for many for the forgiveness of sins."* Jesus poured out his blood; in the Bible blood symbolizes life. Jesus poured out his life so that you may be forgiven and released from guilt. In other words, If Onlys are so deeply imbedded in us it takes the life and death of Jesus, the blood of Jesus to cleanse us.

Are you offended by blood? Do your sensitivities cringe at the idea of blood cleansing you? We worshiped in a church where there was no mention of blood in the Communion service. I asked why and was told that some in the congregation were offended. Offended! So we end up with a bloodless, anemic, insipid religion with no power! No wonder some Christians are guilt-ridden!

197

Our spiritual ancestors asked and sang, *"Are you washed in the blood of the lamb?"* We sing, *"There is a fountain filled with blood."* Is this image crude, gross, primitive, offensive? So is guilt. Guilt is ugly, demoralizing, incapacitating, paralyzing. Guilt is so strong, so powerful, it takes the life and sacrifice of Jesus, the blood of Jesus, to cleanse us. Image yourself standing in a fountain where your If Onlys are washed away down the drain, carried into the sewer where they belong. And leave them there! Don't rummage around in the sewer trying to take back your guilt!

When you receive the bread and wine or juice in Holy Communion, image the body and the blood, the life of Jesus, entering your body, cleansing, forgiving, washing away your guilt, freeing you from the tentacles of the If Onlys, freeing you to walk, to live forgiven and cleansed.

CHAPTER TWENTY-FIVE

Who's to Blame?

As a society, we are heavy into blame. If we can find someone to blame, then we can relax and pawn off the responsibility to someone else, anyone but ourselves, or our comfort zone, or our style of life. If we can blame school shootings on parents, or TV and movies, or video games, then we don't have to assume responsibility for our nation's morals and values.

On a personal level, if we can find someone to blame, we can shirk personal responsibility. Blame mother for alcoholism, blame the teacher for poor grades, blame the government for immorality—then we don't have to accept responsibility.

The Blame Game is a national pastime carried to extremes by the U. S. Congress and widely used in churches! When something goes wrong, when something bad happens, the first response often is "Who's to blame?"

I'm here to help!

Flabbergasted, I couldn't believe her! I had only been in Merced several weeks when Elizabeth (and I knew her name!) came into the office. She was elderly and walked with a cane. I greeted her, "Hi Elizabeth, what's up?" She replied, "Last Sunday, you asked us to write a note on the bulletin, but the pencils in the pew racks were broken, so I have come to sharpen the pencils!" She saw a need, and she filled it! She didn't call the office and storm, "Who's to blame? Who's in charge of the pencils!" She didn't phone the chair of the Worship Committee and complain about the state of the sanctuary! She didn't criticize! She was not interested in finding someone to blame. She took care of the situation!

*   *   *

When a mistake, oversight or a problem occurs, rather than ask, "Who's to blame?" ask, "How can I/we fix it?"

CHAPTER TWENTY-SIX

What About Women?

Are women less intelligent?

In many countries and homes today, women are considered the weaker sex; not only weaker physically, but intellectually as well. Historically, men didn't think women had the intelligence to participate in a democracy, but women used their intelligence, discovered their power and won the right to vote.

Are women persons or things?

Historically, and in many places and homes today, women are treated as property, subject to the whims and dictates of their husbands. In Modesto, a woman came to my office and described the physical abuse she endured from her husband. She had gone for help to her pastor, who told her that her husband was the head of the house and could do as he pleased. Her role was to submit, suffer and endure, like Jesus did on the cross! I told her to get out of the marriage. She did and joined our church! Thankfully, women have now won the right to charge their husbands with abuse, and receive protection from shelters, police and courts.

I received a brochure announcing a new women's movement that was holding huge rallies. It sounded interesting until I read the sentence, "We have received permission from our husbands and pastors." I threw it in the wastebasket!

Are women fit to be ordained?

Historically, women were denied the right to serve the Lord as pastors. I'm proud of our denomination. In 1761, John Wesley, the founder of Methodism, a man way ahead of his time, authorized women to preach. In contrast, there are many denominations today that still do not allow women to serve as clergy, and some don't allow women to serve on administrative committees.

In Modesto, I was visited by a group of Episcopalians who asked to use our chapel to start a new church. I asked why they were leaving. "Because the Episcopal Church is now ordaining women." I told them our church was not interested in helping them. Ironically, one of our associate pastors was a woman!

The Methodist Church began ordaining women in 1956. In 1961, when I was appointed to the newly formed Central Minnesota Methodist Parish, consisting of ten churches and four pastors, one of the pastors was Mary MacNicholl. Formerly a deaconess, she was one of the first women to be ordained. Mary was classic! She wore a black dress in the winter, a gray dress in the summer, rimless glasses, her hair in a pug and a hat. With the Bible under one arm, and the Methodist Book of Discipline under the other, those rural Minnesota Methodists didn't know what hit them!

Are women deserving of salary discrimination?

The law of the land thinks so. Many companies and institutions compensate fairly with equal pay for women, but the current law has loopholes that make it difficult for women to address inequities legally. The struggle for equal pay for equal work continues.

What does the Bible think about women?

Proverbs 31:10-31 is a beautiful tribute to women in the male dominated culture of that day. An acrostic poem, it was written in Hebrew, with the first letter of each line in Hebrew alphabetical order. The woman described is a good wife, far more precious than jewels. She is a hard worker in the home and a business woman. She buys fields, plants vineyards, makes and sells linens. She is a loving mother; strength and dignity are her clothes, and she is wise. Her children call her blessed, and her husband praises her, "Many women have done excellently, but you surpass them all."

In the Old Testament (politically correctly now called the Hebrew Scriptures), some of the leaders were women.

What did Jesus think about women?

Jesus interceded for the woman who was being stoned for adultery. Notice the man had no such punishment. It was the victim's fault, which is still a common belief held by some today.

Jesus denounced easy divorce. In his day, all a man had to do was issue a certificate saying he no longer married. The woman was out on the streets with no rights.

There were no women among the original twelve disciples, but women helped support the mission and played a major role in Jesus' inner circle. According to Matthew, Mark and Luke, when Jesus died on the cross, only a group of women were there to support him. The men were afraid of being arrested.

Was Jesus married? A fragment of a scroll has been found indicating he had a wife, but it has not been authenticated.

Following Jesus' death and resurrection, women played a prominent role in the early church. Jesus' mother was a major player. And when Paul sent greetings to the churches, the lists included women. In Romans 16:1, Paul wrote, *"I commend to you our sister Phoebe, a minister of the church at Cenchrae, so that you may welcome her in the Lord as is fitting for the saints, and help her in whatever she may require from you, for she has been a benefactor of many and of myself as well."*

Early church reversal

From that high point of women's leadership, things went downhill rapidly. Evidently the men were threatened, quickly took the reins and put women "in their place." 1 Timothy 2.9-15, *"Women should dress themselves modestly and decently in suitable clothing, not with their hair braided, or with gold, pearls, or expensive clothes, but with good works, as is proper for women who profess reverence for God. Let a woman learn in silence with full submission. I* (and most biblical scholars don't know who the author is*)* *permit no woman to teach or to have authority over a man; she is to keep silent. For Adam was formed first, then Eve; and Adam was not deceived, but the woman was deceived and became a transgressor. Yet she will be saved through childbearing, provided they continue in faith and love and holiness, with modesty."* Whew! Did the men take control or what!

I don't understand how the author exonerates Adam! After all, Adam ate the fruit. It is also interesting to me that those churches today who deny women the right to teach or have authority usually ignore the rest of the verse, *"dress themselves modestly, not with their hair braided, or with gold, pearls or expensive clothes!"*

Women were not allowed to be priests, and they were not even allowed to sing! So, women organized their own movement and lived together in convents where they prayed, sang to their hearts' content and did mission work. In the Church of England to this day, women do not sing in the cathedral choirs, only men and boys.

In the early Methodist church, women organized their own ministry, and today the United Methodist Women is the largest women's organization in the world! Before women were ordained, the Methodist church consecrated women deaconesses who, like Catholic nuns, were single, taught, did mission work and started hospitals.

In fact, Good Samaritan Hospital in Phoenix was started by a Methodist Deaconess. In 1911, Lulu Clifton arrived in Phoenix to recover from tuberculosis. She only had $12 to her name, but she was convinced that Phoenix needed a new hospital. She began in an apartment building, called it the Arizona Deaconess Hospital, and today it is known as Good Samaritan.

What about the head of the house?

The least understood passage on marriage is Ephesians 5.22-23. Paul wrote, *"Wives, be subject to your husbands as you are to the Lord. For the husband is the head of the wife."* So, the husband is the head of the house and the wife is the foot? A 90-year old woman in my Modesto church liked to say, "He may be the head, but I'm the neck, and I can turn that head any way I want!"

*   *   *

I was pastor in Manteca when a married couple joined the pastoral team. Marilyn was very controversial as no other church in the city would even consider having a woman pastor. Besides that, she did not take her husband's last name! I sang in the choir, and during one practice, a tenor, with another man between us, leaned over and asked me,

"What do you think of her not taking his name?"

"It doesn't matter to me."

"Doesn't the Bible have something to say about that?"

"In the Bible, there are no last names."

"Well, doesn't the Bible say the husband is to be the head of the house?"

Knowing his wife to be a strong, forceful woman, I exclaimed, "Do you mean to tell me you are the head of your house?"

He stuttered, hemmed and hawed, and said, "Well, I would be if I had to!"

*   *   *

The church sign listed the pastors:
Douglas Norris
John Norris
Marilyn Watts
John joked, "Somewhere in there is a married couple!"

*   *   *

But, let's look at the Ephesians passage in greater detail. Most miss the point. Most begin with verse 21, *"Wives, be subject to your husband,"* ignoring the preceding verse, verse 20, *"Be subject to one another out of reverence for Christ."* A mutual relationship.

Verse 25, *"Husbands, love your wives just as Christ loved the church."* How did Christ love the church? Quoting from the Message translation, *"Husbands, go all out in your love for your wives, exactly as Christ did for the church—a love marked by giving, not getting."* Husbands are not told to dominate or rule or abuse, but, following the example of Christ, go all out in love—giving not getting.

Paul continues, verses 28 and 29, *"Husbands should love their wives as they do their own bodies. He who loves his wife loves himself.*" As a husband nourishes and tenderly cares for his body, so he nourishes and tenderly cares for his wife.

In a Christian marriage, each are equal, using their unique gifts and graces for each other. When each puts the other first in priority, both are winners.

What I believe about woman is Biblically sound and in accordance with United Methodist tradition: A woman is a child of God, unique but equal in every way with men. She deserves equal respect and equal opportunity to serve God in the home, church, workplace and society. A woman has the right to make her own decisions, live her life as she sees fit as a disciple of Jesus, and in marriage be devoted to her husband as he is devoted to her.

But more importantly, to summarize, what does the Bible think about women? The decisive, over-riding answer: Paul wrote in Galatians 3:28, *"There is no longer male and female, for all of you are one in Christ Jesus."*

CHAPTER TWENTY-SEVEN

Why Churches Do Not Grow

Many churches, especially United Methodist, are stagnant and declining. The denomination is declining in membership. The question is constantly asked and debated: why aren't we growing? Based on my experiences, here are a few reasons.

1) Often when a pastor is transferred, the new congregation organizes get-acquainted small groups. Among other topics I asked, "What are your dreams and hopes for the church?" In one church, a repeated answer was, "Oh, if only we could hear children in the halls again." When the church started to grow and children were again coming to Sunday School, then we heard the refrain: "The children are eating all the cookies at Coffee Hour!" And we wonder why churches don't grow!

2) A woman wondered what was the purpose of the planning session. I explained that we would be brainstorming as to what we would like the church to be like in ten or twenty years. She said, "I don't care. I won't be here!" And we wonder why churches don't grow!

3) Lyle Schaller, respected church consultant, said that the unwritten purpose of the Board of Trustees is to close the church. All the problems of wear and tear, maintenance

projects, financial difficulties would be avoided if the church closed! Either close the church or turn the buildings into museums. In January when the Trustees (who are responsible for the buildings and property) organized for the year, I challenged them, "When the youth or children's ministry leaders approach you, don't respond with 'How much will it cost? Who will clean and maintain?' But rather ask, 'How can we help?'" It also helps to elect program persons to the Board of Trustees, because they have a broader vision.

4) What also inhibits ministry and therefore church growth is the Landlord mentality. When facing tough financial decisions, a congregation often decides to start renting rooms to outside groups. In my ministry, I discouraged this process and worked to "evict" groups when their lease ran out. Rather than let outside groups conduct preschools or exercise programs, etc., challenge the church to offer the programs as part of the church's outreach ministry. Not only do outside groups use rooms that the church could well use with expanded ministries, the groups gradually come to feel that the property, and particularly storage rooms, belong to them!

5) The Lay Leader was middle-aged and most of the committee chairpersons were his age or younger, so I complimented him on the church's election of younger leadership. He replied, "The old folks have given us the responsibility, but not the authority!" It is difficult for the establishment to move over and make way. I often observed how congregations want younger folk to join their

church . . . until they start coming! Then the reins are withheld. And we wonder why churches don't grow!

I witnessed a classic example of how this works while on vacation. Our van needed an oil change so we stopped at a garage in a small town in Kansas. When I paid the bill, I gave my credit card to the clerk, who was a man of my age or even a little older. He apologized for the time he was taking to process my card, "They put in this new system." It took him longer to process my card than it did to change the oil! Standing at his side was a high school student, probably working in the garage for the summer who, I'm sure, knew how the new system worked.

Do you get the picture? Do you think the old fogey would ask the kid how to do it? The kid offered suggestions; they were ignored. Every now and then the young man couldn't contain himself, and he would reach around the old guy and push a key, but the old man ignored him. Finally, the old geezer telephoned MasterCard and waited until he reached a real live person who talked him through the process with the kid standing there! Why is it so difficult for us to let the younger generation do it?

Growing churches will readily turn responsibility over to whomever has the skill, ability and motivation. Growing churches recognize when something doesn't work anymore. Just because something works with the older generation doesn't mean it works with the younger. But there are many churches dying because they think the ministry is only for the old folks. In dying churches, younger people are welcome as long as they act like the older, talk like old people and do what they are "allowed" to do.

6) I attended a fascinating two-day workshop conducted by Herb Miller, called "Magnetizing and Revitalizing Your Church." He has conducted extensive surveys of growing churches. One survey asked visitors why they came to a particular church. Do you know the reason most often given? 77.9% come the first time because they were invited by someone in the congregation. The difference between a growing church and a declining church is that the members of a growing church invite their friends and families.

The second largest group of visitors, 6.9%, come because they saw the building. 4.2% come because they saw the church ad in the yellow pages.

You might be interested to know how Palo Alto church compared. When I was pastor, I asked people who attended our "Introduction to the First United Methodist Church of Palo Alto" session the question, "How did you learn of our church? Why did you come the first time?" Now, I have not kept statistics, so I can't give you percentages, but the #1 response given by those who eventually joined our church, was the music. Most of the first-time visitors came because of our music program. Many of them first came to a concert and then returned to a worship service. The second largest group of visitors came because they found our church ad in the yellow pages. The third group of visitors came because they saw the building. The smallest group of visitors came to our church because they were invited by someone in our congregation.

Do you see what this says? We were missing out on the #1 reason given why people come to a church. We were missing a huge potential of new people. Why? Our congregation was not doing a good job of inviting people. In growing churches, 77.9% of first-time visitors come because they were invited. Rarely was that reason given by our visitors! Therefore, we were only reaching persons who were attracted by our music program and the yellow pages. Imagine what would happen if church members began inviting people, if they would tap the rich potential in their circles of relationships! Many of their friends are unchurched. Work this question into a conversation, "Do you go to church regularly?" If they say, "Yes," then share experiences. If they say, "No," then say, "I'd like to invite you to mine." Isn't that easy!

Not only do many find it uncomfortable to invite friends to church, many also find it uncomfortable to greet visitors. After I retired in 1999, we traveled for 12 weeks cross-country visiting family and friends, sight-seeing and going to church. I wish I had kept count but in most churches we were ignored. Greeters shook our hands but did not introduce themselves or ask us our names. Most pastors gave us perfunctory handshakes, even though they must have known that they didn't know us. After the superficial greeting time during the worship services, few spoke to us after the service. Two or three times the pastor and a few in the congregation asked our names and welcomed us.

In one church during the greeting time, a couple introduced themselves but after the service said nothing. The pastor shook our hands impersonally at the door. During the service, it was announced that there was a fellowship lunch following the service. I purposely stood near the door of the Fellowship Hall, but not one person invited us to come inside to the "fellowship" lunch. And we wonder why churches don't grow.

Contrast that reception to a church in Texas we had visited years before. After the service, Ellie was invited to the women's group; I was invited to join the men's group and the choir. If we had lived there, we would have joined the groups and the church!

CHAPTER TWENTY-EIGHT

How to Avoid Burnout—
Involved, Yet Detached

How do you love without being consumed? How do you serve without losing your identity? How do you feel the pain of the world without it destroying you? How do you respond to others without becoming too involved in their lives? How do you become involved in people's lives, yet maintain perspective, objectivity and identity?

When God calls us to serve, it is to serve with perspective and objectivity while retaining our identity. When perspective, objectivity and therefore identity are lost, we experience burnout. Involved, yet detached, is the goal of love, neighborliness and Christian service.

When God calls us to serve, the ideal response can be lost to extremes. At one end of the spectrum, we do nothing; we can't be bothered. We are quite content to live self-centered lives, looking out only for ourselves and our own welfare.

At the other end of the spectrum, we sincerely respond to the call to serve and then proceed to get too involved. We burn out, consumed by the task.

Some parents are too involved in their children's lives. Some parents are not involved enough, but some are too involved. They even try to take their child's place in the dentist's chair! They are over-protective, make all the decisions, violate any sense of privacy and smother their children.

Some Christians get so involved in church work or in social causes, they lose their identity, perspective and energy. They burn out. Some spouses lose their identity. They no longer have any goals, dreams or life of their own. Some women have found the world to be too threatening, so they allow themselves to be consumed by their husbands. They live vicariously through his name, his goals, his career. I doubt if God calls anyone to the sole vocation of help-mate, lost in service to the other.

A Japanese wife of an American serviceman caused quite a stir on the air force base by her devotion and attentiveness to her husband's every need. She waited on him hand and foot. However, on the day she received United States citizenship, when her husband sank into his easy chair and called for his slippers, she announced, "I'm an American citizen now. Get them yourself."

How do you become involved in people's lives, yet maintain perspective, objectivity, and identity? How do you become involved in peacemaking, ministry to the homeless and hungry, justice causes without burning out? How do you become involved without being swallowed? How are you involved, yet detached?

Is detachment too strong a word? By detachment I mean the art of loving, befriending, working for social justice and peace, without being consumed. By detachment

216

I mean the art of being involved without losing perspective, objectivity, and identity. We look to our model, Jesus, for example and guidance. No one can be more loving, self-giving, dedicated to people and their welfare than Jesus. Yet, Jesus practiced detachment in at least five ways.

1) Jesus knew about **organization**—how to divide the task into steps and accomplish one step at a time. When Jesus sent the twelve disciples out to the villages to preach about the kingdom of God and heal the sick, he carefully took them through steps. He trained them, giving very explicit details, even telling them what to wear, what to pack. He taught them what to say. He anticipated difficulties they might encounter and taught them how to handle conflict. He divided the large task into measurable and definable intermediary goals.

Management talk sounds familiar to us, but do we practice it with our families and in our personal lives? What we have to do sometimes seems so overwhelming but make a plan, step by step, and the tasks cease to be so overwhelming.

Practice detachment by detaching yourself from anxiety over the entire journey, task, or problem, and deal with it one step at a time. Hopefully, there is a sense of reward and accomplishment for each step. "A journey of a thousand miles begins with one step," is ancient Chinese philosophy. And we might add, the journey continues with one step at a time.

2) At times Jesus needed **space**. At times he needed to get away from the crowds to regain perspective on his

mission. He would then go into the wilderness on a retreat. Sometimes Jesus took his disciples with him, or a few of them. Sometimes he went alone. Jesus detached himself physically and mentally by finding space. Go on a personal or group retreat. Walk to Emmaus, a weekend experience that is life-renewing and life-changing.

One morning at 10:00, I needed space. I had to get out of my office and out of the church! I told the Administrative Assistant I would be back. I got into the car, drove a few blocks, stopped the car, pulled out a piece of paper and wrote down 14 decisions I had made in the two hours I was in the office—some I classified as crises! After the break, I returned to work.

My favorite "space" was at the ocean. Often I took a one or two night mini-retreat to a motel in Santa Cruz or Pacific Grove.

3) Jesus practiced the rhythm of involvement-detachment-rest-prayer-renewal-reinvolvement through the keeping of the **sabbath**. Early America similarly kept the sabbath. In our modern, complex, stressed, pressurized culture, we have lost the sabbath; and by losing the sabbath, we have lost detachment. In order to keep a sense of perspective, we each need to detach ourselves weekly from the daily routine and pressures, worship God with our church family, and then spend the rest of the day resting. No cleaning the house, doing the laundry, mowing the lawn, sneaking back to the office or working on a laptop. We need to rest our minds, rest our spirits and let them catch up to our bodies.

4) Jesus knew the importance of **fun times**, special moments of relaxation and even indulgence. John 12:1-8 includes a saying of Jesus which has caused lots of interpretation trouble over the years. Jesus said, *"The poor you have with you always."* Was Jesus resigning himself to the inevitability of poverty? Was Jesus giving us a way to cop out of our responsibility to care for people? Jesus' words have been used by some to undermine efforts to combat poverty.

What did Jesus mean? What I think he meant is so simple the scholars probably dismiss it. Look at what was going on. Jesus was in Jerusalem. Now called Holy Week, it proved to be his last days on this earth. Opposition was growing. There were plots to take his life. Jesus needed to detach himself from the hostile scene. He needed a time of relaxation, a time to be with friends so he and the disciples walked to the village of Bethany to the home of Mary, Martha, and Lazarus. Good friends. They had a party. Mary washed his feet with expensive oil. We don't practice foot washing anymore because we wear shoes but, in Jesus' day, after a long walk on the hot sand, washing one's feet provided a moment of pleasure and joy. Mary added to the joy.

Judas reprimanded her for wasting costly oil on Jesus' feet when the money could have been given to the poor, which, of course, Judas would not have done. Have you noticed how often those who oppose spending money that could be given to the poor, don't give money themselves! What I think Jesus is saying is: yes, give to the poor; yes, get involved in ministering to the poor; but there are times when it is necessary to detach ourselves, relax, indulge a little and be renewed. It's okay to go out for a nice dinner. Jesus is talking about balance.

5) Jesus practiced the art of **ultimate detachment** and detached himself from his own life. He gave his life for us. Hebrews 12:2, *"For the joy that was set before him, he endured the cross."* Detachment means to cut ourselves loose from attachments, attachments to things and possessions. Detachment means we possess nothing and nothing possesses us. In Philippians 3:8, Paul wrote, *"I count everything as loss for the surpassing worth of knowing Christ Jesus my Lord. For his sake I have suffered the loss of all things, and count them as rubbish, that I may gain Christ and be found in him."*

Look at it this way. If tomorrow your house burned down and you lost all your possessions, would it really matter to you in the long run? What is really important? If you can free yourself from undue concern about things; if you can detach yourself, you free yourself from much anxiety, stress and "possessiveness." Likewise, if you should die tomorrow, would it really matter to you in the long run? If you can free yourself from undue concern about your physical being; if you can detach yourself from your physical life, you free yourself from a great deal of anxiety and stress.

Then, free of worry about yourself, detached from things, finding moments for space, rest, prayer, and fun with family and friends, you are free to really love your

220

friends, spouse, parents and children. You are free to become involved in doing good and worthwhile things, yet retaining perspective, objectivity and identity.

CHAPTER TWENTY-NINE

How to Tell a Need From a Want

"Be subject to one another out of reverence for Christ."
(Ephesians 5:21) We are called to submit to one another in
mutual submission, not one always the "submitter" and the
other always the "submittee." We submit to one another,
we serve one another when one is in need. Serving is based
on need. Sometimes you are the needy one and need to be
served; sometimes the other is the needy one, and you
submit. You are both giver and recipient. We are both
people-feeders and people "needers." Rather than
submitting to one another on the basis of gender where the
woman submits and serves the man; rather than submitting
to one another on the basis of color where the person of
color submits and serves the white; rather than submitting
to one another on the basis of economics, where the one
who "doesn't work" submits and serves the "provider," the
Christian style is mutual submission, where we submit to
and serve one another on the basis of need.

But how do you tell the difference between a need and
a want? Does Christian service and submission mean we do
whatever is asked of us, whatever is expected of us? How
do you know when the need is genuine and you are not
being manipulated? Some women feel like maids because

their husband and children want to be waited on. Is she not a good wife and mother when she asserts herself and differentiates between a need and a want? Just because the children want service, does that want justify their mother becoming their maid?

A child may want to eat candy but needs to eat vegetables. A child may want to be cared for and protected but needs to experience responsibility. A child may throw a temper tantrum, screaming on the floor in the middle of a store. The child wants attention and is manipulating for attention. But the negative behavior should not be reinforced by giving it attention. Wise parents know children should not always be given what they want, but the question is how does the parent know the difference between a want and a need? How do you know what is a need? Are we really helping people when we submit to their wants? Are we really helping people when we participate in their sickness rather than contributing to their health?

We are advised not to give cash to those who ask for help. What they want is cash. What they need is assistance in getting their lives together. Rather than giving cash, send them to a service agency who will feed them, help them find short-term employment and housing which may involve the use of our facilities, and counsel them. An alcoholic wants a drink. An addict wants a fix. You are not a good friend or spouse or Christian servant when you give them what they want. The point is: you do not necessarily help your children or your spouse or your friend by giving them what they want.

In Acts 3:1-10, Peter and John differentiated between a need and a want and responded to the crippled beggar's need rather than his want. Peter and John went to the temple at the ninth hour—3:00 p.m.—to pray. This was the third prayer time of the day. A lame man was at the gate of the temple called Beautiful asking for money. The handicapped were supported in those days not with SSI checks, but by begging. This man, and we don't know his name, was born crippled and every day was carried to his place at the temple door. When he saw Peter and John, he asked them for cash. Peter stopped and looked directly at the man. No doubt he was pleased to receive attention. "Perhaps the kind gentlemen will be especially generous." He looked at them expectantly, but he did not get what he wanted. He did not get what he expected. He did not get what he asked for.

What he received was the caring and loving act of Christians who responded to his need and not to his want. What the man needed was healing. He needed help to stand on his own feet and walk. Peter said to him, *"In the name of Jesus Christ of Nazareth, stand up and walk."* Peter reached out, took him by the hand and lifted him up. Immediately his feet and ankle bones received strength. The man went into the temple with Peter and John walking, jumping with joy and praising God.

What we see here is the goal of Christian love and action. When you love someone and want to help him or

225

her—neighbor, spouse, child, friend, stranger—the goal is to help her or him walk, jump with joy and praise God! What we all need in our lives are people who will encourage and help us walk, jump with joy and praise God. What we may want, and what we do not need, are well-meaning do-gooders in our lives who keep us emotionally crippled—dependent, defeated, empty of confidence, filled with self-pity.

* * *

To help differentiate between a need and a want, consider the long range results of your actions and ask yourself these questions:

1) Will what I do help them become self-reliant and independent or more dependent on others? Will they learn to walk with head erect or be emotionally crippled, dependent on others? I can still recall the scene in the play, *The Miracle Worker*, where Anne Sullivan taught blind and deaf Helen Keller how to eat. It was literally minutes where I sat on the edge of my chair, barely breathing, watching a woman and a little girl wrestle, hit, slap, kick. Anne would pick Helen up, seat her on the chair, put a spoon in her hand and guide the food to her screaming mouth; without the sound of the screaming, of course, which made the scene even more dramatic. All I could hear was the sound of the scuffle. Some would call Anne cruel. Helen's mother coddled Helen, protected her, waited on her and felt sorry for her in her handicap. The love of Helen's parents left Helen crippled. The tough love of Anne gave Helen Keller

life. As a result, Helen Keller walked, jumped and praised God!

In Manteca Church, a three-year old blind girl was a student in the Head Start Children's Center. The teachers were excellent. They followed the principle: don't do anything for her she can do for herself. This meant that the girl often stumbled, ran into things and fell. But we watched that blind three-year old girl gain confidence. She laughed, she learned, she loved. She walked, jumped and praised God! Don't do anything for people, including the elderly, they can do for themselves. When you do, you increase their dependency and decrease their self-reliance and self-esteem. Don't do anything for people they can do for themselves, except for moments of celebration. Making the child's bed to surprise him or her is sometime a fun thing to do; but as a rule, don't make the child's bed when she or he is old enough to do it for themselves, which is probably age three. Don't pick up clothes lying around the house, including the spouse's. Walk on them as if they aren't there, and refuse to do any laundry that is not in the basket. THE GOAL IS SELF-RELIANCE AND INDEPENDENCE.

2) Will what I do help them develop relationships of mutual respect, or will what I do encourage them to manipulate others to submit and wait on them? Back to the children throwing the temper tantrum in the middle of the store. Because they know how to embarrass you by picking a public place in which to throw a tantrum, do you yield to the manipulation, pick them up, coddle them and perhaps

bribe them with candy if they will just shut up; thereby encouraging them to lose respect for you and to treat you with disrespect by manipulating you? Or, do you walk away to another part of the store where the children cannot see you? They will soon quit because you are not responding and because they now become the center of the public's attention, which they have not really bargained for. Similarly, do you allow yourself to be manipulated by your spouse's or your friend's pouting and sulking? Or, do you walk away to another part of the store and wait for the spouse or friend to exhibit more mature, respectful behavior? THE GOAL IS MUTUAL RESPECT.

3) Will what I do help them face reality and live their lives honestly and responsibly, or will what I do encourage them to tell themselves lies, develop a distorted view of life, and blame others for their troubles and predicaments? When youths get into trouble with the school or with the police, do you try for a cover-up? Do you intercede and try to protect them from the consequences of their actions? Or, do you let them face the music and learn how to live their lives responsibly and honestly? When you are quick to bail them out, you are probably bailing them in and contributing to their irresponsibility, and an irresponsible person who is bailed out by others has a very difficult time learning how to walk, jump with joy, and praise God. THE GOAL IS RESPONSIBILITY.

4) Will what I do help them gain self-confidence, or will what I do encourage self-pity and helplessness? A child falls. You can see it's not a serious fall, no danger of

228

broken bones. Do you run, pick the child up, wipe away the tears and say, "Oh, you poor thing. That nasty sidewalk," which encourages him or her to be dependent on you, manipulate you for attention, and blame others or situations like the sidewalk for their problems. Or do you say, "Come on, you can make it," and wait while he or she pick themselves up, which may sound cruel, but actually contributes to the child's self-confidence and self-reliance and gives them a sense of victory because they can now pick themselves up, walk and jump with joy. THE GOAL IS SELF-CONFIDENCE.

5) Will what I do help inspire faith and commitment to Jesus Christ, where they will live their lives in loving service to one another, and praise God in gratitude, thankful for their lives, rather than blaming, bitching and griping that nothing is ever right. THE GOAL IS A GRATEFUL, CHRIST-CENTERED, UNSELFISH LIFE OF SERVICE.

To sum up, all five questions can be stated in one: Will what I do help people to walk, jump with joy and praise God, or will what I do hurt them by helping them become emotionally crippled and handicapped?

One further point. Remember what Peter said when he helped the crippled man to walk, jump and praise God. Peter said, *"In the name of Jesus Christ, walk!"* You are not alone. Commit your actions to Jesus Christ. I Corinthians 10:31, *"Whatever you do, do to the glory of God."* Rely on God to help you make the right decision.

Rely on God to help you differentiate between a need and a want. Trust in God to bless your actions.

CHAPTER THIRTY

How to Change God's Mind

Can you change God's mind? Is it possible to change God's will? Is it possible to alter circumstances and situations? Can the irrevocable become revocable? Can the given become a beginning rather than an ending?

Too many answer, "No!" A sense of hopelessness is widespread. Too many people say, "This is the way I am. I can't change. It's hopeless." Even teenagers with their entire lives ahead of them sometimes give up and feel, "This is my personality. I can't change. I can't get out of this hole." Addicts to drugs and alcohol feel hopeless. People who feel the world is against them think things can't change.

There are hopeless Christians who feel that God has already decided how things will be and that it is hopeless to try to change God's mind. Many believe the will of God is immutable, unchangeable. Some even believe that God's will was set in concrete eons ago and that we are all predestined to be who we are and do what we do. With such a belief, the believer's lot in life is to accept the inevitable, be content with what happens, acquiesce, surrender, submit, don't complain and be quiet! Prayer, to them, is surrender rather than asking God to change things.

Jesus taught us to persist. Jesus taught us not to acquiesce and surrender to what happens to us, but to persist in determining what happens. In Luke 11:1-13, the disciples asked Jesus to teach them how to pray, and Jesus taught them what we now call the Lord's Prayer. Then he gave an example of prayer. What do you do when friends from far away land unexpectedly in the middle of the night, and you have no food in the house? Remember, when Jesus told this story, there were no convenience stores open 24 hours a day.

What do you do? You go next door, pound on your neighbor's door and ask to borrow some bread. The neighbor hollers, "Hey, are you crazy? It's in the middle of the night. My kids are asleep. I'm trying to sleep. Come back in the morning."

So now what do you do? Should you accept the situation and send your guests to bed hungry? Should you accept the given? Should you acquiesce to the will of the neighbor and give up?

Not according to Jesus. Do you know what Jesus' advice is? "Keep pounding on the door!" Keep pounding until the neighbor in exasperation, gets out of bed and loans you some bread. And Jesus said the neighbor will give you the bread, not out of friendship, but in order to shut you up, so everyone can get to sleep. And Jesus says, that is what prayer is!

Jesus also told about a woman who kept pleading with the judge for her rights, pleading with the judge to grant her plea. The judge ignored the woman, but she kept coming and kept pleading. Finally, the judge granted her request because, he said, "She will wear me out." Jesus said that is prayer. Prayer is hounding God until God relents and grants the request, saying, "She will wear me out."

Yes, God's mind can be changed. Yes, God's seemingly immutable will can be altered. Yes, situations and circumstances can be changed. Continuing in Luke 11:9-10, Jesus urges, *"Ask, and it will be given you; seek and you will find; knock and it will be opened to you. For everyone who asks receives, the one who seeks finds, and to the one who knocks, it will be opened."*

Ask, says Jesus. Ask, and it will be given you. Do you believe God not only hears our prayers, but answers them? Ellie was bringing my mother home from her radiation treatment. While driving on the freeway, Ellie prayed that my mother would not be sick. As she prayed, suddenly a feeling of deep peace and a burst of energy came over her. Later in the day, Janet, our Church Administrator, called Ellie and asked if she could do anything.

"Just pray."

"Oh, we did pray in the staff meeting this morning."

"Was that about ten to eleven? I knew someone was praying, and it felt like more than one person." Coincidence? Or, did God gather their energies together with the Holy Spirit and focus God's healing spirit on them at that time? Prayer changes things.

*   *   *

Miryl had a chronic arthritis condition. For two weeks, she had unbearable pain. Nothing would touch it. She couldn't sleep for seven straight nights because of the pain. Sunday noon she was sitting on her patio when she felt the pain lessen. It gradually faded and proved later to be a turning point. She began to sleep at night and the next Sunday worshiped with us. Was it a coincidence that at the time her pain lessened, several of us, including her daughters, were gathered in the chapel for the monthly healing service praying specifically for Miryl? One of her daughters has since said, "I don't know if Mother's recovery was due to the prayers or her medicine, but let's not give up on either one!"

"Ask," said Jesus. Pray. You are not necessarily stuck with your circumstances, your life, your relationships or your personality. Don't surrender to hopelessness. When you feel discouraged, when you feel life is dealing you a raw deal, when you are unhappy with your circumstances, when you feel you can't change your life, ask, pray, persist and go for it!

Sometimes we get discouraged with the slow speed of social change. Will people of all colors and national origins be given fair chances? Today, with the rise of conservative reaction, with the onslaught of skin heads, neo-nazis and ultra right-wing movements, the advances made in civil and human rights might be lost. When you get discouraged and are tempted to give up your social causes, remember the dogged persistence of the neighbor knocking for bread, and the woman pleading with the judge, and take Jesus seriously and literally, "Seek and you will find."

Now I'm not saying there are no limitations. The famous serenity prayer which Alcoholics Anonymous has adopted to inspire its members, reads,

God grant me the serenity to accept the things I cannot change,

The courage to change the things I can,

And the wisdom to know the difference.

Yes, there are some things that cannot be changed. Don't give up too easily. Don't acquiesce and decide too soon what cannot be changed. Take courage to change the things you can. Don't stop pounding on the door too quickly. Don't become discouraged too quickly.

Jesus did not say life would be easy. No, overcoming handicaps, overcoming disappointments, overcoming setbacks and failure, developing your skills, changing poor attitudes, keeping your eyes on your goal are not easy. But don't give up too soon. Ask; pray with all your might. And seek. Pray and work. You shall overcome.

CHAPTER THIRTY-ONE

Oh, How They Laughed!

Let me out!

It was the first Sunday in my first appointment after seminary, and I was excited, nervous and apprehensive. After leading worship in two of the country churches, I arrived at the Milaca Church just in time for the 11:00 service. By that time, I needed to use the rest room. No one saw me when I ran into the vestibule and downstairs to the rest room. When I shut the door, the handle fell off on the outside, and I couldn't open the door! Just then I heard the Hammond organ begin the prelude upstairs. I banged on the door and hollered. Finally, the only maiden lady in the church came down to "stop the kids from making all that racket." I called out, "Pick up the handle. Put it in the door and open it, please." She did and told no one about it, but I did several months later. Oh, how they laughed!

One day I visited one of our elderly members in the nursing home. She, a merry soul, was about 90. Having heard the story, she rocked back and forth in her rocking chair, chuckled, and asked, "Was she playing *Blest Be the Tie That Binds?*"

Cotton puffs

In Zimmerman Church, we held a rollicking, very successful five-day Vacation Bible School one summer. Isobel invited the teachers to lunch and served home-made cream puffs for dessert, except mine was filled with cotton! Oh, how they laughed!

It's the carrots!

A few months after we arrived at St. Paul's Church in Manteca in 1974, the church's Couples' Club had a Saturday dinner in a Lodi winery. The tables were set with wine glasses. The winemaster lectured and explained what wine went with each course

Before we ate, there was silence in the room. No one lifted a glass; they were trying hard not to stare at Ellie and me. I took my sweet time, enjoying the discomfort, but finally lifted my wine glass and took a sip. An audible sigh was heard around the room as they all relaxed, drank wine and enjoyed their dinner.

Towards the end of the meal, I made my way to the restroom. Frank called out, "What's the matter? Can't hold your liquor?" I impulsively said the first thing that entered my mind, "Actually, it's the carrots!" They laughed. Next morning in church when I went to the pulpit, there lay a carrot! On one Sunday, I took a swallow of water during the sermon, not noticing until it was too late, the olive in the water. Oh, how they laughed! Manteca St. Paul's Church was a happy church!

A genuine potluck

The Wranglers, a senior citizen fellowship group at St. Paul's, held a monthly potluck. One month there were two desserts and everyone else brought baked beans! They were embarrassed, but I loved it. Oh, how I laughed and so did they. But it was a long time before anyone brought baked beans again That was a real potluck—none of this A-F bring salad, G-N bring a main dish, O-Z bring a dessert!

The letter

While I was in Japan and Ellie was teaching in Minnesota, we exchanged many letters. One of mine included a proposal. In 1957, who would have considered a trans-Atlantic phone call! At Ellie's 60th birthday party, oldest son Jack claimed he had found the letter and proceeded to read his made-up version. He began the letter with the weather. Oh, how the crowd laughed, but the actual letter did begin with the weather! As we wrote to each other throughout the three years, the assumption was gradually reached that we would marry. The actual letter was the final step in the decision.

She didn't!

When I was a student at Garrett, Dwight Loder was the President and later became a United Methodist bishop. His son David was in Ellie's study hall at Evanston Township High School. 25 years later we entertained the Loders and the Stuarts (our bishop) at Sunday dinner in Palo Alto. Bishop Loder had quite a sense of humor. While we men were visiting and watching a football game, he got up, stormed into the kitchen and laughingly said to Ellie, "I remember you. You were the waitress at the Stillwater Lowell Inn who dumped that tray of chicken dinners on me!" Oh, how we laughed.

It is a small world. 15 years later when we moved to Walnut Creek, California, David became our dentist.

* * *

At a baptism, the parents interrupted me as I was saying the wrong name. I quickly responded, "When did you change her name?" Oh, how the congregation laughed!

Lair of the Bear

Wesley Church holds an annual Family Camp at Pinecrest Lake in the Sierras every Labor Day weekend. Knowing it was going to be cold, I took my heavy Stanford sweatshirt. On the way, realizing I had forgotten to bring a cap, we stopped at a Walgreens, grabbed a Stanford cap and purchased it. The next morning I went into the dining room for an early cup of coffee and was almost thrown out! I had not computed that we were at the Lair of the Bear, a campground owned and operated by the University of California at Berkeley, chief rivals of Stanford. Begging for my life, I explained that two sons had graduated from Stanford. It was all in fun but do check out the environment! Oh, how the Wesley folk laughed!

CHAPTER THIRTY-TWO

Into the Future

In 2011, on the occasion of the 50th anniversary of graduation, Ellie and I, along with classmate Dave and his wife Sandra, traveled to Garrett for the weekend events combined with commencement activities.

While there, David Heetland, Vice President of Development, suggested that Garrett-Evangelical Theological Seminary establish the Douglas and Eleanor Norris Scholarship Fund. Flabbergasted and overwhelmed, we immediately declined. In the next few weeks, however, we considered the implications, asked advice from family and trusted friends and decided there was no downside. If the $25,000 minimum was not received to guarantee the endowment, whatever was raised would be put into the general scholarship fund. So we said, "Let's do it!"

I had received a scholarship while at Garrett, and appreciated it immensely. We were introduced to the donors and developed a relationship with them. We worshiped with them at their church, dined at their apartment on Lakeshore Drive overlooking Lake Michigan; they visited us in Minnesota and California, and we corresponded with them until their deaths many years later.

Without assurance that the scholarship would be endowed, on August 7 a celebration of my 60 years of uninterrupted ministry and the announcement of the Douglas and Eleanor Norris Scholarship Fund was held at the First United Methodist Church of Palo Alto, California. David Heetland came from Garrett to make the presentation in the worship service. The Family Camp Singers sang, many friends attended and our sons prepared barbeque tri-tip for 300.

Since then, generous contributions have been and are continuing to be received from family, friends and members of churches I have served. The $25,000 was reached in a matter of weeks, and the fund is growing. At the end of the second year, it had doubled. An annual scholarship from the endowment is awarded to a student seeking to become a pastor in the United Methodist Church as her or his first career. Our fantasy dream is to grow the scholarship to eventually provide a full tuition. The profit from the sale of this book will be added to the fund.

Currently Garrett's tuition is $18,000 a year, plus books and housing. We have stipulated that the scholarship be awarded to students pursuing the United Methodist pastoral ministry as their first career. Many graduating students leave college with a student loan debt. I wonder how many look at an additional substantial seminary debt, wonder how they would pay off the debts on beginning pastor salaries and give up.

Believing strongly in the future of the church, and knowing that the church needs the best, it is our prayer that

242

this scholarship fund grow to provide a significant difference to a student answering God's call to the ministry.

Garrett-Evangelical is a United Methodist seminary with ecumenical commitments. More than four hundred students representing nearly forty different denominational groups are enrolled each year. The residential campus in Evanston is at the geographical center of Northwestern University. The seminary is committed to preparing bold leaders for the church, the academy and the world. The purpose statement is "to know God in Christ and, through preparing spiritual leaders, to help others know God in Christ."

It was heart warming to receive a letter from our scholarship recipient expressing gratitude for the blessing received because of aid from the scholarship. If it weren't for the scholarship, enrollment at Garrett would have been impossible. The knowledge that our scholarship fund is enabling students to pursue their dream of ordained ministry makes it all worthwhile.

CHAPTER THIRTY-THREE

All in the Family

It was my joy and privilege to:

- Baptize my Mother
- Conduct the wedding ceremony for my Mother-in-law Ellen and Ed
- Lead all three sons and their brides in the Saying of their Vows
- Sing "The Lord's Prayer" at each wedding
- Baptize all our grandchildren—Alison, Adrienne, Erin, Julia, Melanie, Sara, Amanda, and Tyler (our only grandson!)

I'm grateful to the pastors who invited me to participate in the weddings and baptisms.

*   *   *

Jack and Tim were born in the 15-bed hospital in Milaca. The bill for each was $75, including the doctor. When I mentioned this at Family Camp, someone hollered, "You get what you pay for!" Craig was born in St. Louis Park in Methodist Hospital. That bill was $300. But, no amount of money can purchase the joy and pride we have in our three sons. They are successful, generous, talented, friendly, creative, gifted men, and loving, supportive fathers. They enjoy life; they laugh, play and work with great enthusiasm. And, they all are active in their churches—each have held responsible positions.

*   *   *

On January 24, 2001, beautiful twin girls, Julia and Melanie, were born to Barbara and Tim in Scottsdale. Frightening us at two weeks, listless Julia with blue lips, was rushed back to the hospital with RSV (respiratory syncytial virus) and put on oxygen for a week. Melanie was also hospitalized in the same room.

During their first four months, it was Ellie's joy to be with Barbara to help take care of the twins four days a week.

On Mother's Day with the immediate families attending, I baptized Julia and Melanie during the 9:30 worship service.

I have baptized hundreds and the only infant to cry was my granddaughter Sara!

That Starry Night

"Tell them about Jesus" continues in our family. Our youngest son Craig, his wife Laura, and daughter Sara have written a delightful children's Christmas musical called *That Starry Night.* The original music and script are built around the Nativity story which I adapted. The musical was first performed in the First United Methodist Church of Palo Alto in 2012 on Christmas Eve. Sara and Tyler were "stars." It is available for use in other churches. Paradise Valley United Methodist Church performed it in 2013 where granddaughter Amanda was a "star."

My Dad

I tell you about my Dad in the hope that you will consider the impact and influence of your parents on your life, and I hope that learning about my Dad will encourage you who are fathers or hope to be fathers someday. Fathers are important people in a child's life.

My Dad was not perfect. It may surprise you but perfection is not a universal characteristic of or qualification for fathers (or mothers either). I suspect that most children want and expect their parents to be perfect. Some become quite disillusioned when they discover imperfections in their parents. Maturity comes to us when we realize our parents are not perfect, but we accept them anyway! I have lived through an era when our culture has been very hard on parents. Popular psychology put a great deal of blame on parents. It was considered therapeutic to list Dad's faults and blame him (or mother) for our problems. I confess I went through that exercise with my Dad, and how healing it was for me to write this reflection, accept his imperfections and give him credit for all I have learned from him.

One thing about my Dad I did not like was his smoking. I disliked the stinging in my eyes and the smell of cigarette smoke, especially the smell of old smoke from filled ash trays. I learned to eat rapidly, so I could leave the table before he lit up and covered the table with smoke like a blanket. On the other hand, I realize now that my Dad was eating with us and that phenomenon is not all that common in American homes today. My Dad's smoking finally did him in. He developed a terrible cough, so he switched to chewing snuff. Yes, righteous me considered that equally, if not more, offensive. He developed cancer. His stomach was removed. The cancer spread to his esophagus, and he died relatively quickly.

I learned how to die from my Dad. I flew to Arizona to spend a few days with him in the hospital and to be of support to my mother. He apologized to me for being too poor to provide for us as he would have liked. It is very important for persons who lived through the great depression to be good providers. I was flabbergasted and told him I never realized we were poor. I told him I had everything I ever needed, and certainly I never felt inferior to anyone.

We flew our boys down to see my parents the next weekend. My boys not only loved their grandfather, they enjoyed him. He had a wonderful sense of humor and loved to tease and play with them. My brother flew down to see him and then my sister. Our Dad told her, "I'm ready now. I'm going to stop eating." My sister, thankfully, did not react, but accepted his decision to speed up the dying process. She wisely told him, "Do drink water, though. Dehydration is not pleasant." He did. In a matter of days, he died—peacefully, with dignity and style. I do believe each of us has the right to die. Because of our paranoid laws, the right to die on her terms was denied to my mother, but that is another story. Incidentally, the doctor discovered a spot on my mother's lung caused by second hand smoke.

My Dad was not a churchman. He was raised in a strict Baptist home and rebelled by not going to any church. Have you noticed how the Lord has a sense of humor? My poor Dad, trying so hard to be rid of church, had to contend with his Baptist father, his oldest child a Methodist minister, his other son a committed Christian in an Assembly of God Church, and his daughter a faithful Roman Catholic! My Dad never ridiculed or criticized me for my interest in church; in fact, he drove me to Sunday School and Youth Fellowship when the neighbors couldn't.

My Dad worked his way through the University of Minnesota and graduated with a business degree. This was during the Great Depression and the only work he could find was with the Highway Department. When I came along, he returned to the family farm with my mother, lived with his parents (which I learned in later life was very difficult for my mother), and resumed farming, which my Dad hated. How tragic it must be to work day in and day out doing something you don't want to do, but have to do. But he made the best he could of his life. He did not feel sorry for himself, nor did he become cynical. When the war came (World War II, not World War I!), he held two jobs—a farmer and a guard at a munitions factory. After the war, he gave up farming and both he and my mother became Psychiatric Aides in Anoka State Hospital. Both seemed to enjoy it. My Dad worked well with people and he was well liked at work and in our community.

My Dad served his community, and I realize now I was very proud of him. I was proud to be a Norris and to be known as Glenn Norris' boy. He was a member of the School Board and served as clerk. He kept the minutes and wrote out the checks that the treasurer then signed. I remember watching to see how much the teachers were paid and was amazed to see that some of them received $100 a month! He also served on county committees and once made a speech to the entire school assembly. I was proud! Children want to be proud of their Dad.

My Dad was also very proud of me and supported me in every way he could. Whenever I did something public in school or in church, my Dad and Mother were there. Parents, never underestimate the importance of being present for your children. I acted in several plays and my proud Dad was always there. I realize now I must have disappointed him with my lack of interest and ability in sports, but he never showed his disappointment. He enjoyed sports and was on a winning baseball team in his younger days. He played ball with me, but never let me know how terrible I was. In fact, my Dad never put me down. Oh, once someone said to him, "I hear your son is a good singer." My Dad replied, "Yes, good and loud!" But I considered that comment the truth and in fun, not a put-down! I don't sing any softer either!

My Dad taught me responsibility, which is lacking in many homes today. If a child doesn't learn how to be responsible for their life, what future is there for them? I must admit it is easier to learn responsibility on a farm than in a city. It is obvious to a child on a farm the effects of not doing the chores. The chickens get hungry when not fed. The cows moo and moo when not fed. You can see how full the udders get when they are not milked. If the snow isn't shoveled, the car can't move. My Dad never hit or spanked me. He was gentle, but I knew what was expected.

My Dad also taught me to follow through. He taught me to keep my word. When I was in eighth grade, I was elected treasurer of the Sunday School. My Dad helped me set up a bank account. The offerings were not much, $2 or $3 a Sunday, but it was an important job. At the end of the first year, the books wouldn't balance. I was a few dollars short. I wanted to quit, but my Dad wouldn't let me. "You took the job, you complete it." I don't remember him helping me balance the books because it was my responsibility. What he did say was, "Make up the difference yourself." So I took my hard earned money (and on a farm I earned an allowance; I also mowed a neighbor's big lawn without a power lawnmower and was paid $1) and made up the difference. When my term as treasurer expired, there was an excess, so I took some out! I still lost money on the deal, however!

One of the great gifts my Dad gave me was his love for my mother. He was not an affectionate person; he was a typical Minnesota farmer. I don't remember him hugging me or my mother. But my parent's love for each other was clearly evident. They were faithful with never any hint of extra-marital affairs. They enjoyed each other's company. I can still see them sitting at the table drinking coffee, talking and talking. They were also good neighbors. We had a wonderful neighborhood with lots of sharing of tasks and lots of card parties.

My Dad was generous, but he enjoyed giving the impression he was tight with his money. He was extremely frugal, but generous when it was appropriate. When he died, I carried his ashes back to Minnesota. I conducted the memorial service, our son Craig played the organ, and my sister, brother and I sang a trio; so we didn't have to give honorariums to the pastor, organist or singers! My Dad would have appreciated that! Besides that, the grave digger didn't show up, and we had to reschedule the burial. Then he got mixed up and almost dug the hole in the wrong place. When he did find the Norris plot, he measured by stepping it off in farmer style. "Oh, about here," he said. When I asked him how much we owed him, he said, "Sorry I was late. It's on the house!" My Dad must have really enjoyed that!

My Mother

My Mother made the best of it. Within a strong network of family and friends, she worked hard, played heartily, and died without fear.

From my Mother I learned the importance of family and friends. She was born the second oldest in a family of nine. Seven have died, including one infant. The remaining brother and sister are a closely knit, supportive family yet today. Most Sunday afternoons in my childhood, when we weren't going to baseball games, we spent with my Mother's family playing cards. When a teenager, I recall playing Norwegian Whist with my grandfather and two uncles all night long. My grandmother made us breakfast!

My Mother and Dad also had several close couple friends with whom they visited, traveled, went to dances and out to eat. Our farm neighborhood was also closely knit. The women had a club which met monthly and there were frequent card parties. We all need a network of caring, concerned people who will love us in spite of our faults. It does take a village.

My Mother was a hard worker. As the second oldest, she learned at an early age how to cook, launder, sew, clean, garden, farm and care for her younger siblings. Life was not easy on a Minnesota farm, especially on her family farm which was on poor sandy soil. I remember her telling me what a joy it was when they had sugar to put in the cake they baked. My Mother learned from her mother the art of taking nothing but a few leftovers and making a feast. She made the best of it. My Mother was also a captivating story teller as was her father, my grandfather. When they both got to reminiscing, I would sit there for hours with my mouth open.

She married my father during the Great Depression. My Dad worked for the highway department until I was born. They then were forced to return to farming, which my dad did not enjoy. They moved in with his parents. My Mother was caught in the middle, caring for me on one hand and my grandparents on the other. To my Mother's credit, I never realized the tension under which we lived until my Mother shared late in life. She made the best of a difficult situation. She had to do all the cooking, laundering, gardening and cleaning, and take care of me and my grandmother when she became ill with tuberculosis. Evidently my grandmother was not easy to live with, but my Mother never let on how difficult her mother-in-law was.

I loved my grandparents dearly. My Mother did not put me in a position where I had to take sides. When you compare photos of my mother at age 70 with photos of her at age 30, she looked younger at age 70. It was not easy for her but she accepted the hand dealt her and she made the best of it. Without sour grapes, commiserating, self-pity, anger, or bitterness, she made the best of it.

She treated others with respect, giving them the benefit of a doubt. In her quiet, gentle way, she put the best connotation on anyone's suspect behavior, even making excuses for them. She was a peacemaker and made the best of every situation.

My Mother especially enjoyed playing cards. The latest game, which her family is still playing, is "Hand and Foot," a version of canasta. Our oldest granddaughter is named for my mother. Alison Beatrice at age four, like her great-grandmother, played Crazy Eights. Alison wanted to win all the time but her dad patiently explained that if you are going to play cards, you must learn how to lose. We do children no favor by manipulating situations so they always win. Cards, when you don't cheat, can teach patience, how to lose, and how to win graciously!

My Mother also enjoyed picnics. I remember going on lots of picnics. We didn't need tables either. We would lay out the tablecloth on pastures or beside lakes and rivers, and all of us would play in the water. Even in her later years, when we visited my parents in Arizona, we went on picnics in the Arizona desert. She also enjoyed rock hunting in the desert. After retirement, my parents spent six months in Minnesota and six months in Arizona. They learned how to play shuffleboard in their Apache Junction mobile home park, and one year my Mother was the Arizona State Champion in shuffleboard. Even though my Mother worked hard, she knew how to play. Play helped her make the best of the hand she was dealt.

My Mother died without fear. She was not reared in a church and did not go to church while I was growing up and living at home. Whenever they visited us in California, they went to church with us and in her later years in Arizona, she began going to a neighborhood church. When she confessed her faith, repented of her sins, and accepted Jesus Christ as her Lord and Savior, it was my joy and privilege to baptize her in the Palo Alto church.

After my father died, my Mother developed cancer. When it was not possible for her to return to Minnesota for her last summer, she lived with us for her final seven weeks. Ellie and she had bonded in a special way the weeks before our marriage when my parents invited Ellie to drive with them cross-country to meet me in Seattle when I returned from the three years in Japan. Sharing the back seat, my Mother confided in Ellie the unhappy experiences she endured with her mother-in-law. Through the years, Ellie cherished my Mother as a role model and friend.

In her final days, Ellie was her caregiver and did a magnificent job. Our network helped considerably. For the last month of my mother's life, Ellie did not cook one meal. The doorbell rang and there would be someone from our Palo Alto church family with a meal. Before my Mother slipped into unconsciousness because of the morphine, she was awed by the outpouring of love. She kept asking, "How can we thank them?"

When the radiation no longer had any effect and our doctor, who was also a close friend, told her he could do nothing more for her but give her morphine for the pain, my Mother called her brothers and sisters, called my brother and sister, told them all she belonged to Jesus and said, "Goodbye." Then she courageously sat up in bed, without any fear of death, and said, "Call the doctor. I want a shot. I'm ready." My Mother wanted to die as she lived her life—in dignity. But we had to explain how our society no longer allows doctors to exercise compassion. She died a horrible death without fear; but also, without dignity.

Because of my Mother and many other deaths I have witnessed as a pastor, I was one of the signers for the Right to Die initiative on the California state ballot. I believe strongly that people who are terminally ill, with a prospect only of pain, have the right to die in dignity, surrounded by their loved ones.

CHAPTER THIRTY-FOUR

My Faith Journey

According to James W. Fowler in his excellent book, *Stages of Faith, The Psychology of Human Development and the Quest for Meaning*, the first stage of faith, characteristic of young children, is **fantasy and imagination.** As a child, I had a vivid imagination. Growing up relatively alone on a farm, I played imaginary games. I made up stories and acted out all the parts. My grandparents played card games with me, read stories and told me the family stories. I learned to read at an early age and have long been fascinated with books. This was in the pre-television era when radio was the medium. My favorite radio program was "Let's Pretend," 10:00 on Saturday mornings.

Reflecting on my childhood, I realize how blessed I was to have parents and grandparents who allowed me to express my imagination. I was never repressed or squelched. I learned that the world is an exciting place, a fun place, full of adventures waiting to be explored. According to Fowler, children at an early age find an awareness of death and sex and soon learn about the strong cultural taboos. I remember when I was about six years old, my cousin and I were caught in the haymow exploring each other's bodies. Her mother spanked her. My parents let me talk about it. I remember telling them all about the differences between boys and girls! I recall my Dad deeply concentrating on the food he was eating, raising his head every now and then to glance at my Mother! My parents were open, gentle, tolerant and accepting.

As I reflect on my early home life, I realize how fortunate I was to be reared in a nonjudgmental home. Rarely was anyone, including me, criticized or demeaned. My parents rarely raised their voices and I was only spanked once when I went across the road to the neighbors. My Mother was afraid for my safety. There was very little prejudice in our home. On Valentine's Day my Mother made sure that I took valentines for every child in the classroom. No one was left out. When the first black family moved into our school district, just a few miles from us, and the children rode the school bus with me, it never entered my head not to be nice to them. I am grateful to have been reared in an atmosphere of openness and acceptance where I was allowed my freedom—freedom to imagine, freedom to explore, freedom to learn.

According to Fowler, the second stage of faith development is the **literal** stage. Here we begin to take on the stories, beliefs and observances for ourselves, and we interpret them very literally.

Conscious faith at this stage of my life was a simplistic world view based on a very literal view of the Bible. I was a fundamentalist in my high school and college years. Especially was I intrigued with end-of-the-world theology.

I read everything I could get my hands on about biblical prophecy and was sure that Jesus would be coming soon. Hitler was the Antichrist and Russia was the Bear of the North prophesied by Ezekiel. For recreation, my group of friends would jump in a car and go to Minneapolis to the Billy Graham crusade meetings or Pentecostal revivals. I liked the peppy, rhythmic music and the enthusiasm.

I was rigid in my theology and biblical interpretation at this time, but I was not rigid in my personality and outlook. My parents' openness and tolerance were reinforced by the Methodist Church. I am so thankful God led me to that church. I can still see the faces of many of those dear folk who called me "Dougie" and loved me along with all the children and youth. They tolerated our misbehavior. They were loving, open people. I had four special friends in junior and senior high school. We were called the Four Musketeers and roamed the hallways of the school and the streets of our town. They were all taken to church regularly by their parents. They were great friends, and we shared fundamentalist beliefs, but even then I appreciated the open, loving, accepting, tolerant atmosphere of my Methodist Church. I loved my church, and I loved going to Sunday School, morning worship, and Methodist Youth Fellowship in the evening. I never missed; I wouldn't think of being absent.

When I was a sophomore in college and the District Superintendent appointed me to pastor the two small, rural Methodist Churches, I preached my literal theology with vigor. The District Superintendent called me "Billy

Sunday." I had a wonderful three years. We had youth groups of over 25 kids in each church. We played, sang, laughed and prayed. Faith for me was a joyful, confident experience. I had accepted Jesus Christ as my Lord and Savior. I knew I was born again. I was given self-confidence and leadership skills, and I preached with fervor. The folks in my two churches and in my home church all hoped that I wouldn't lose my fire in seminary.

While a missionary in Japan, I entered the stage of faith Fowler calls the **reflective** stage. There I began to demythologize my literal theology. Actually, the demythologization had begun earlier and was gradual. I remember in high school asking my Dad where Cain and Abel found wives to marry when Adam and Eve were the first people on earth. He told me the creation accounts were stories not to be taken literally. I found that disconcerting, but pondered it. And in Japan, living in a different culture far from the Bible belt, I began to expand my world view.

It was in Japan at the age of 22 that I learned that my country was not perfect. That was a significant discovery. I also learned that not all the news of the world is printed in our newspapers; that we are not always told the complete story and that not every public statement by our officials can be believed. I developed a world-view that had a sense of realism about my country and my religion. I had the world placed in a neat box with a ribbon around it and now was having experiences, meeting people and learning things that would not fit into the neat box.

Some folks never leave the literal stage of faith. They find it meets their needs and never seem to question. Others, however, find themselves questioning their assumptions, and the subsequent crumbling of their faith is often a devastating experience. People who find their understanding of the world and their experiences in the world no longer fitting into their narrow doctrines and literal interpretations have three alternative courses of action:

1) Some prefer to stay with their faith and ignore the conflicts. They have neatly compartmentalized their faith from their daily life. They can profess a belief in creationism on Sunday, carry out their work during the week predicated on evolution, and see no conflict.

2) Some reject all religion. I recall having conversations with two men whose wives are active church members, but they could not bring themselves to join the church because they had rejected the literal faith of their adolescence and had not found a substitute. They were not able to enter the reflective stage of faith development and have thrown out the baby with the bath.

3) Some are able to enter the reflective stage, separate symbol from literal, and formulate a world-view and a theology that are compatible, mutually stimulating and supportive. In my faith journey, I was able to enter this stage with relatively little emotional trauma. Because of the openness of my home and my church, I was able to accept new ideas more easily than those who are reared in a narrow, strict, judgmental atmosphere. By this time, my

faith was more than intellectual doctrines, more than expressions of belief about the world and God. By this time in my life, faith was a way of life—a state of being. Faith in Jesus Christ was a personal relationship with God that transcended belief systems. The imaginative, exploring nature of my childhood sustained me and I found my missionary experience in a different culture and my subsequent seminary training, exhilarating, stimulating and expanding.

I call my faith stance at the present time **open-ended**. My beliefs are not closed but are constantly changing. They are in process. Developing and designing one's theology is a life-time experience, an exciting process as new discoveries, new ways of looking at things are assimilated—sometimes rejected, sometimes adapted, sometimes adopted. With a solid background in biblical studies and trust in the indwelling Holy Spirit, I have confidence in my ability to discern. I can explore. I have attended far-out seminars. I participate in workshops of which I know nothing. I am not afraid of new ideas or new thinking because I have confidence in discernment. I am open to life, confident that God will keep me in the faith. Faith is not just an intellectual exercise, faith is a way of life. The **fourth** stage of development is when faith becomes a way of life with an open-ended belief system.

CHAPTER THIRTY-FIVE

Where Is God?

I'll go . . . God sends, yes, but God also leads.

Where is God? Of course, God is everywhere. Jesus said, John 4:14, *"God is spirit."* God is not a person, place or thing. God is not a noun. God is spirit. God is energy and, of course, God the Spirit is everywhere—above, around, within. But I find it difficult to relate to everywhere. Everywhere is too nebulous. I personally cannot get a handle on everywhere. The key question is: where is God primarily located?

We were created to be in relationship, in covenant, with God. We hunger and yearn for fellowship with God but many don't know where to look. Traditionally, people have looked above and within. The theological terms are immanence and transcendence. There have been debates for centuries. Is God primarily immanent—within us—or is God primarily transcendent—outside, above and beyond. The preacher said, "Reaching God is like dialing a number on a telephone. The telephone is your heart and you dial God's number." An elderly woman interrupted, "Tell me, would that be long distance or a local call?" Of course, God is both transcendent and immanent, both out there and in here, both above and within.

Transcendence

Through much of history, the transcendence of God has been emphasized. For many people, God is located "up." We point up to heaven. God looks down. People climb mountains to be closer to God. Churches and cemeteries were built on the highest hill in town or in the open country. Jerusalem is located in the mountains so there are many biblical passages urging worshipers to ascend the hill to reach the Lord. Church buildings, especially cathedrals with high ceilings, point up to God, and when they couldn't afford a high ceiling, they attached a spire or steeple to point up and out to God.

But science has taught us there is no "up." What's up is down in a few hours. I remember looking at slides of the sky made by an amateur astronomer preacher. He said that he had found heaven. There's a gap in the sky, an absence of stars, near the North Star. I was quite impressed until I took astronomy in college and discovered that the poor guy didn't have a large enough telescope!

In various biblical accounts, the transcendent God sent angels as messengers to intercede between God and humans. Today, many who emphasize the transcendence of God, believing that God is in the distance, pray to Mary, the mother of Jesus, or saints to intercede for them.

The temptation with believing that God is primarily way out there, watching from above, is that we then tend to feel that God is removed from us; that God is not involved in our daily struggles and pains; that God wouldn't understand or doesn't have time to relate to us. It is also tempting to believe that because God is way out there, above us, we don't have to deal with God. Some try to live their lives as far removed from God as possible.

When God is above, prayer is difficult. Sometimes the believer feels that God is so far away that his or her prayers never leave the room. When my maternal Grandpa was dying, he wanted me to pray with him, because he felt that his prayers didn't leave the room. I didn't know enough at the time to tell him his prayers didn't need to leave the room because God is right here.

Immanence

The other tradition emphasizes that God is "in"—within each person. The theological term is "immanence." The Greeks used the word "soul," and spoke of the "spark of divinity within each person." Quakers speak of the "light of God" within each person. When you look for God within, prayer then is meditation rather than communication with a transcendent God.

The temptation with believing that God is primarily within each of us is that God may become very subjective. The temptation is to identify God with our personal interests, desires, and conscience. The temptation is to look solely inside us, and become absorbed with ourselves. As a result, it is tempting to lose sight of God as judge. The thrust of biblical faith is lost. The heart of biblical faith is covenant. God enters into covenant with us where God offers unconditional love that is never canceled. Our response is to be faithful followers, to be God's people belonging wholly to God. The temptation with believing that God is primarily within is that the covenantal dimension is often lost. It is difficult to establish a covenant with something inside us.

Now, let me make myself perfectly clear! I hope you are not misunderstanding me. Of course, God is above and beyond. Of course, God is transcendent, the Judge. God is far beyond our comprehension. God transcends our limited experience.

And, of course, God is within. Meditation is a very dynamic experience with God when we get in touch with the indwelling Spirit of God and when we listen to the voice of God within us. But, is God primarily transcendent or immanent? Where you look to God is of critical importance to your understanding of God, your understanding of life, and your understanding of yourself.

Ahead

May I suggest another image—an image which is very helpful to me and, I believe, an image that is true to the Bible. I encourage you to experiment with this image. Let it roll around in your head. I believe God is ahead of us. God is ahead of us, calling us to follow. According to Mark 1:14-20, when Jesus began his ministry, his first act was to recruit disciples. And what he said to them was, *"Follow me."* Can you see Jesus walking through the Galilean countryside with the disciples behind him, talking as he walks, calling over his shoulder, "Come on, guys, follow me!"

Paul wrote in Philippians 3.12-14, *"Forgetting what lies behind and straining forward to what lies ahead, I press on toward the goal for the prize of the heavenly call of God in Christ Jesus."* It's like driving a car. Don't spend most of your time looking in the rear view mirror. Enjoy the windshield with its panoramic view of what lies ahead. Don't dwell on the past. Look ahead.

God called Abraham to leave his comfortable home in what is now Iraq, *"Go from your country...to the land that I will show you."* God led Moses and the slaves from Egypt through the wilderness to the Promised Land with the sign of the fire by night and the cloud by day. Jesus set his face to go to Jerusalem, facing the future undaunted and unafraid even though he knew he would be put to death. The New Testament anticipates and looks ahead to the day of God's victory, the coming of the kingdom.

Jesus is ahead of you, calling you, urging, "Come, follow me into the future. Follow me. I need to use your hands, your feet, your talents to do my work, to bring justice and peace." God tugs and pulls on us. You've felt the tug. God doesn't let us be satisfied with ourselves. When we think we've finished, God opens up another whole arena of things to do. God won't let me stay retired. Jesus says, "Come on, follow me and be an interim pastor." My response? I'll go . . .

On those mornings when you don't want to get out of bed, Jesus says, "Come on, get up. I'll go ahead of you. It will be a day filled with opportunity, a day filled with glory and joy." Jesus goes ahead, preparing the way, pointing out the potholes, warning, "Don't go there! Follow me!"

When you are told the dreaded word "cancer," God is ahead, preparing the way, comforting, saying "Don't be afraid. I am with you." When you are near the valley of the shadow of death, Jesus goes ahead to prepare a place for you.

God is ahead, calling you to grow; not to hibernate or stagnate.

God is ahead, calling you to struggle with yourself and the world, not to escape into a peace of mind nirvana.

God is ahead, calling you to sing and dance, not to mope and feel sorry for yourself.

God is ahead, calling you to follow, not you telling God what to do.

God is ahead, calling, leading.

God is ahead, calling you to follow. Will you answer, "I'll go"?

CHAPTER THIRTY-SIX

Tributes

Through the years, I have received tributes that are humbling, but I offer a few to give insight into and perspective on my style of ministry.

*   *   *

From a Milaca Church member:

Doug and Ellie are super people. Milaca has so many memories of this family, we could write a book. He came to Milaca when our church was at an all time low. He taught us to share, love and how to progress. With him, our desires were great. He always set our goals at the top. One could not be a loafer with this eager young man around. That's how we grew.

*   *   *

Excerpts from the Palo Alto Church newspaper, June 28, 1974:

Dear Doug, you always 'leavened' a room when you entered—the atmosphere was more interesting and exciting. . . . You're different now from when you came from Minnesota—you have sideburns and keep on your shoes during meetings (mostly). . . . And then I must not forget the time that the United Methodist Women got two positions filled right after church on Sunday as a direct result of your sermon, so they testified.

And preaching. Don't all of us have a "favorite" stashed away in our heads, garnered from the many rich and warm sermons Doug preached? Many members commented with amazement on his ability to reach out to the congregation— each of us feeling Doug was speaking right to us and wondering why he was leaving all those other guys out! How many jobs did he preach YOU into?

Ellie—sparkle—concern—living life at its best. Doug—on call during the night for a troubled teen-ager— understanding alcoholism as an illness—supportive of others' new responsibilities, patient with changes—how could we have endured the years without his ready smile, joke, hug—troubled times with his constant loving help— wiping tears away. In the offices there was always a current joke—usually traceable to Doug—and his laughter rocked the church. No matter where you were at Hamilton and Webster, you knew if Doug was in the building! And always there was singing.

Doug is a hard working administrator, able to organize order out of chaos, accompanied by joyous music wherever he is.

It's FUN to work with Doug. (Note: when Ellie read this she snorted, "I hope they don't ask if you're fun to live with!")

Letter received as we left Manteca Church, June 30, 1981:

Dear Doug,

Words seem very inadequate for my attempt to express the complexity of thoughts and feelings that are surfacing just now. . . .

St. Paul's was the setting in which I first experienced a joyful worshipful happening. . . .

There were really times when your words on Sunday morning were so much more than words. Doug, in those early months of my arrival, this all happened midst many tears. Then there was more journeying. The sermon in recent weeks that stands out as an absolute classic was "The Spirited Christian." Many of the concepts presented that morning were integrated at a deep level for me. . . .

Then I reflect on the counseling hours so generously given in love and concern.

I think especially now of each member of your family as well—Ellie, and her beautiful, direct approach to living and loving. Jack, and his comfortableness and manner of allowing others' special qualities to shine forth. Tim, and his openness of sharing as he grew personally, and his willingness to go the extra mile in encouraging another of like age. Maybe the fruit can't always be seen but Tim certainly planted the seeds. Craig has given to all of us so freely of his musical talents, and I feel I was just beginning to see Craig, the unique growing young man.

*   *   *

271

From the Merced Church Lay Leader:

I want to express my appreciation to you for what you are doing in our church. . . . I appreciate your very positive attitude and the way you express it. I give you a lions share of credit for our church coming out in the black, and paying all our debts, including our apportionments this year . . . I concur with the many others who have mentioned to me that you give very fine, inspiring and thought provoking sermons. We need to continually hear about "Yeesus" you have a special way of telling us. . . . Several talked about appreciating your sense of humor. It is also a very fine quality you have of meeting problems head on and making the difficult visit right away when it is needed. I like that you give us, your parishioners, a challenge, not allowing our church to become complacent. Being an excellent pastor is a special gift you have.

*   *   *

(The following was written by 12-year old Kaytie in 1997, while I was pastor in Merced. It is typed on a white/blue sheet of paper, and adorned with five colorful hot air balloons.)

Pastor Doug

My friend Pastor Doug is a really neat guy. He loves God and everyone around him. He has a temper fuse about 3 miles long. Pastor Doug is very good at bringing things into perspective. His sermons are touching. Sometimes you go home bawling your eyes out, and sometimes you're really charged up. He has raised three wonderful children and is a loving husband.

Being tall, but not too tall, Pastor Doug has good posture and a short neck. He has a kind of victorious walk like he's just won a battle. It's probably because he has such good self esteem.

Pastor Doug is probably best know for his great sense of humor. I'll never forget the time that a bunch of friends from our church were at a party. It was being held at a friends house whose carpet was new and white. So naturally we all took off our shoes to be polite. During the party we all noticed that there was quite a large hole in Pastor's sock. His birthday just happened be the next Sunday, so after church we had a birthday party. We all ended up giving him socks for presents. I think he figured we were trying to tell him something.

This great man is the most caring, sensitive person I know. He always says things like "great to see you" or "super." But I think the most famous thing he says is "I've been on a trip." That's because a couple of years ago he took a trip to the holy land and for 8 or 10 weeks after that he made a big deal (as a joke) about going on a trip.

My Pastor is a great guy. He is the most fun-loving, gentle, kind, and cooperative person I know. He loves children very much and has a gift for music. He has the most beautiful voice and truly believes what he sings. He loves our church and deeply cares about his congregation. He's had a very exciting life. . . . His sermons touch people in ways he may not even know. We love him so much and are truly blessed to have him as our pastor. He's such a positive person and I want to be like him.

*   *   *

(The following article appeared in the 2008 pictorial Directory of the Wesley United Methodist Church, San Jose, celebrating my 18-month interim as senior pastor. The article has photos on three sides—serious and humorous photos.)

Thank you Rev Doug and Eleanor!

Retired and hauling "stuff" to new digs in Mesa, Arizona, Rev. Doug got the call. It was a Call from above and he and his lovely wife Eleanor, of 49 years then, turned their car around and headed back west to be our interim Senior Pastor. Just a short-term appointment six months, the Bishop promised. Just until January 2008.

January came and went and he remained steadfast and loyal to this new Wesley family he had become fond of serving. He and Eleanor felt immediately at home, comfortable in their welcome here. Never in their lives had they even encountered the likes of a Wesley pot luck and they were overjoyed. We do like our food fests and do like to fellowship. We're indeed hopeful that all our potlucking didn't lead to his physical hardships of late.

He rolled up his shirt sleeves, and immersed himself. Of course, he's used to the fire, having been an interim pastor several times before. He got involved in every aspect of the church, its ministries and its memberships, and provided guidance, leadership and vision. He accepted the challenge, listened intently, asked everything, and the church has continued to grow under his leadership. And why? One of his many gifts is his easy-going "fire-side-chat" kind of manner, his warmth and openness and we were all immediately put to ease. He fills the room with joy, laughter and delight.

From the pulpit, Doug's messages, liberal and thought-provoking, sparked discussion and interest as he outstretched his arms and reached outward to encompass everyone with Jesus' message of love, acceptance and forgiveness. While this is a transition period for us, in the time he's been with us, we have grown in affection and love for this tall, lanky Minnesotan in our midst.

We are fortunate and truly blessed Doug answered God's call, as he has served us well, helped us to bloom and flourish, become a dear friend, and prepared the way for our next Senior Pastor.

ADDENDUM

Chronological Order of Ministries

1952-1955   Cedar and West Bethel Methodist Churches, Minnesota

1955-1958   Short-Term Missionary, Nagoya, Japan

1958-1961   Garrett Theological Seminary, Evanston, Illinois (Rocksprings, Harvey, Redeemer)

1961-1966   Central Minnesota Methodist Parish (Milaca, Santiago, Glendorado, Estes Brook, Zimmerman)

1966-1969   Aldersgate Methodist Church, St. Louis Park, Minnesota

1969-1974   First United Methodist Church of Palo Alto, California

1974-1981   St. Paul's United Methodist Church, Manteca, California (Australia Exchange)

1981-1983   First United Methodist Church of Modesto, California

1983-1993   First United Methodist Church of Palo Alto (again)

1993-1999   United Methodist Church of Merced, California

1999   Retirement

2000   St. Luke's United Methodist Church, Fresno, California

2001	Paradise Valley United Methodist Church, Arizona
2003	Mission Bell United Methodist Church, Glendale, Arizona
2007-2008	Wesley United Methodist Church, San Jose, California

I am still open and responding to "I'll go . . ."—preaching, teaching and leading Family Camp.

I retired from active ministry June 30, 1999. The six years in Merced went by quickly. On June 23, my last Sunday, the congregation hosted a fabulous farewell dinner and program. My family had sneaked into my computer, downloaded sermons and announced the new website—dougnorris.com, sermons since 1988.

All profits from the sale of this book will be contributed to the Douglas and Eleanor Norris Scholarship Fund at Garrett-Evangelical Theological Seminary, 2121 Sheridan Road, Evanston, Illinois 60201.